An Introduction to Written Pleading

An Introduction to Written Pleading

2nd edition

Professor Robert Black, K.C.
The Hon. Lord Braid
Sheriff Lesley Johnston
Dominic Scullion, Advocate

EDINBURGH
University Press

Edinburgh University Press is one of the leading university presses in the UK. Publishing new research in the arts and humanities, EUP connects people and ideas to inspire creative thinking, open new perspectives and shape the world we live in. For more information, visit www.edinburghuniversitypress.com.

Previous edition published in 1982 by The Law Society of Scotland
Second edition 2025

Edinburgh University Press Ltd
13 Infirmary Street, Edinburgh EH1 1LT

Typeset in 11/13 Baskerville MT Std
by Deanta Global Publishing Services, Chennai, India

A CIP record for this book is available from the British Library

ISBN 978 1 39951 389 0 (hardback)
ISBN 978 1 39951 390 6 (paperback)
ISBN 978 1 39951 391 3 (webready PDF)
ISBN 978 1 39951 392 0 (epub)

Contents

TABLE OF CASES

TABLE OF STATUTES AND
STATUTORY INSTRUMENTS

Foreword

Spare a thought for young Richard Mylward. So offended was the court by his pleadings which ran to 160 pages when 16 might have sufficed, that he was imprisoned, fined and paraded through the Westminster courts 'bare headed and bare faced' with the pleadings hanging around his neck.[1]

That was 1595.

In 2024, judicial exasperation takes a different form but regrettably continues to be commonly expressed. It is expressed with great reluctance, often after hours spent staring cross-eyed at impenetrable pleadings, having scribbled copious notes, drafted numerous mind maps and having exhausted the ink of every available highlighter pen. The pleader inevitably starts on the back foot when eventually the proceedings call before a weary judge, anxious to make some meaningful progress for the litigants but finding herself hamstrung by incoherent and unintelligible averments.

A good pleader, on the other hand, has mastered the art of making a positive first impression. Their concise, clear and focussed pleadings have assisted the same judge enormously. The good pleader is met with a judge who readily understands what their client wants, why and on what legal basis they should get it.

[1] *Mylward v Weldon* [1595] EWHC Ch 1.

So, you want to be a good pleader? This second edition of Professor Robert Black's *An Introduction to Written Pleading* is an excellent place to start. Whether you are a trainee, newly qualified or a seasoned practitioner in need of a refresh, this handbook provides a step by step guide to pleadings. If you follow its sound advice, you are likely to serve your client's interests well, while also escaping the wrath of the judiciary.

The original book was published in 1982. Over 40 years have passed and while there have been many changes in the practice and procedure of the Scottish courts, the fundamental requirements of pleadings have remained largely the same. The second edition has revised, updated and enhanced the original, most notably, with the addition of a new chapter on special causes (personal injuries actions, commercial actions, family actions, petitions, summary applications and simple procedure) and one which explores the importance of ethics including the pleader's duty of candour.

Lord Braid, Sheriff Johnston and Dominic Scullion, advocate, deserve great credit for distilling a technical subject-matter into a readily digestible form and for honouring the original book by doing so with a lightness of touch and a sense of humour.

Sheriff Principal Anwar K.C. (Hon.)
Glasgow, February 2025

Preface to the second edition

The first edition of this book was published in 1982. In approaching this second edition, we have endeavoured to retain as much of the text from the first edition as was possible. Where sections have been updated and new chapters added, we have tried to emulate Professor Black's writing style and to keep the text conversational and light-hearted, but informative. Where we haven't succeeded in matching the professor's wit, the blame rests entirely with him.

Many people were interested in and encouraged this little project along the way and to them we are most grateful. But in particular, we record our thanks to: the Dean of Faculty, Roddy Dunlop KC, for encouraging the project at the outset and for being a sounding board; Sheriff Principal Aisha Anwar K.C. (Hon), for making invaluable suggestions to an earlier draft and for providing the foreword; and Ysabeau Middleton, Devil Advocate, for commenting on what we thought was the final draft and for dispelling that notion with red pen.

We have attempted to state the law and practice as at January 2025.

DS, PJB and LJ
Aberdeen and Edinburgh
17 January 2025

CHAPTER ONE

Introduction

In 1913 the federal judicial authorities in the United States were engaged in revising the procedural rules applicable to equity cases. They sought advice on reform of their rules of procedure and pleading from a number of eminent lawyers within and outwith the United States. One of those consulted by Mr Justice Lurton, the chairman of the drafting committee, was the then Lord Chancellor of Great Britain, Lord Loreburn. In his reply to the Americans, the Lord Chancellor said this: 'It may be worthwhile for Mr Justice Lurton and his coadjutors to consider the Scottish method of pleading which, in my view, is the best'.

Had Lord Loreburn's experience of the Scottish method of pleading been derived not from the dizzy heights of the House of Lords but from daily modern practice in the sheriff court, his views might, today, be different. Even by 1973, a less rosy view of the Scottish system of pleading was taken by Lord Diplock in *Gibson v BICC*:[1]

> My Lords, when I first became a member of your Lordships' House I was unacquainted with the niceties of the Scots system of pleading. Since then my acquaintance has grown; so has my disenchantment.

Although Lord Diplock offered a somewhat lukewarm recantation in *MacShannon v Rockware Glass Ltd*[2] it is hard to imagine

---

[1] *Gibson* v *BICC* 1973 SC (HL) 15 at 27.
[2] *MacShannon v Rockware Glass Ltd* [1978] AC 795 at 815.

that his disenchantment would have been dispelled had he been commenting in the present century. Whatever one thinks of the Scottish system in principle, it is hard to deny that the general standard of written pleadings, in the sheriff court at least, has not greatly improved since the first edition of this book was published some 40 years ago. *Macphail* writes:[3]

> The need for clear, concise and focussed pleadings cannot be over-emphasised. Unsurprisingly, judicial exasperation is commonly expressed when the court is faced with poor pleadings. A regrettable practice of unnecessarily lengthy pleadings which obscure rather than clarify the issues has developed. Such practices are to be avoided. A clear understanding of the principal rules of pleading … will equip pleaders to better serve those instructing them, and also assist the court in performing its function.

The standard does not seem to have improved in recent years. For a recent example of (justified) judicial exasperation (and an example of how pleadings ought not to be done), see *Parks of Hamilton (Townhead Garage) Ltd v Deas*,[4] in which Sheriff Principal Anwar trenchantly, but pithily, observed:

> The respondent has purchased a vehicle which she claims is not fit for purpose. The towbar has a height in operation of 500mm. She claims that the vehicle cannot be used to tow a caravan, the height of the towbar being too high for that purpose. She claims that the vehicle was supplied with various other defects including a mis-aligned door and mis-matched paint shades (with which complaints this appeal is not concerned). She seeks to reject the vehicle and claims repayment of the purchase price and other losses. Her claim is a straightforward consumer claim, the likes of which are commonplace in the sheriff courts. Her claim is capable of being articulated and answered in a few brief paragraphs.

---

[3] Macphail, *Sheriff Court Practice*, 4th edn, by A Cubie et al (2022) at para 9.43.

[4] [2022] SAC (Civ) 18, 2022 SCLR 292 at para 44 ff. See also *Gutcher v Butcher* [2014] SC KIRK 54 for some equally trenchant criticism.

Yet, the Record in this action extends to 31 pages. The pleadings are disorganised and simply bewildering. Simple matters, such as the use of a defined term for the vehicle, appear to have been incapable of agreement: the respondent refers to the vehicle as 'the car' while the appellant refers to the vehicle as 'the Used MIG Vehicle' …

This is a consumer action. It is capable of being articulated and answered in simple and brief terms. Parties should consider putting their pleadings in order by deleting unnecessary, superfluous averments.

This tendency for pleaders to over-complicate essentially simple disputes is a common theme. As Lord Justice Clerk Dorrian said, still more recently, trenchantly and pithily, in *King v Black Horse Ltd and Others* (another case which began life in the sheriff court), at para [4]:

To say that the pleadings are a mess is to make a statement of extreme generosity to the drafters thereof, in respect of all parties. Somehow they have managed to extend pleadings for this simple scenario to a record of about 80pp. It is abundantly clear that no-one has taken the time to analyse the circumstances of the case in terms which clearly specify the alleged legal consequences said to arise out of the facts, the legal duties which follow, or to specify clearly the remedies sought and their basis. The Sheriff's restrained observations as to the pleadings are stated thus:

'To say that I found the format and content of the Record confusing may be to understate the position. "Bloated" may be a fair description of the pleadings. It contained many typographical errors.'[5]

The 'simple scenario' referred to by Lady Dorrian was that the pursuer had rejected an allegedly defective motor vehicle, due to a non-performing diesel particulate filter; and the principal issue was whether post-rejection use barred the pursuer from pursuing remedies under the Consumer Rights Act 2015.

---

[5] *King v Black Horse Ltd* [2024] CSIH 3, 2024 SLT 135 at para 4, per a somewhat-less restrained Lord Justice Clerk (Dorrian).

It will be seen that endeavouring to avoid over-complication isn't just about acting in the best interests of your client; it is also about self-preservation. After all, having your homework marked in public is never a pleasant experience, least of all when the Second Division of the Court of Session is the marker.

Why should the standard of written pleadings be so poor? Why should 'simple scenarios' at least in factual terms – the pursuer bought a car; it was defective because of A, B, C; the car was rejected; the losses sustained by the pursuer were X, Y, Z – result in pleadings which are so bloated and difficult to follow? The draftsmanship of pleadings by counsel is normally (but not invariably) of a somewhat higher standard – as, of course, it should be.[6] Even the rawest recruit to the Bar with the most gleaming white wig will at least have spent their eight or nine months' spell of devilling being trained in, among other things, the art of pleading summons, defences and minutes of amendment, and duly having them torn apart (and frequently torn up[7]) by their devilmaster, as well as undergoing more formal training as part of the much-lauded Foundation Course run by the Faculty of Advocates. As with most of the other skills which a lawyer must have, so with written pleading; there is no substitute for practical experience and the criticism of one's first faltering footsteps by more senior and battle-scarred members of the profession, preferably before one ventures into a court and suffers the criticism of the judge. That said, while there may be only a limited amount that you can learn about written pleading from books, it is striking that despite several textbooks on the subject (not to mention the first slim edition of this book) the standard of pleading in the sheriff court has scarcely improved. The same mistakes continue to be made, as the recent judicial *dicta* quoted above amply demonstrate.

---

[6] But for a recent example of an exception, see *Livingston Football Club v Hogarth* [2023] CSOH 71, 2023 SCLR 172 (yet another action which began life in the sheriff court), in which the pleadings were described as obfuscating, rather than clarifying, the pursuer's position.

[7] At least in the old days of paper.

Although more than one hundred years out of date, Lees, *A Handbook of Written and Oral Pleading*[8] still contains many useful nuggets for the would-be pleader. While the basic function of pleadings has not changed in the last century, it has evolved as new procedures have developed demanding a different approach.

The aim of this book is to deliver up-to-date advice and guidance on the technique of written pleading. The principles are the same, whether in the Court of Session or sheriff court. We will look, in turn, at the considerations which apply to the drafting of initial writs (or, in the Court of Session, summons and petitions), defences, adjustments and minutes of amendment. We will also consider the different approach which must be taken in certain types of procedure, including commercial actions and personal injuries actions and Court of Session petitions. We set out some cardinal rules, as well as drawing attention to potential pitfalls, many derived from our own (and other people's) mistakes.

But, whatever the forum and whatever the nature of the writ being drafted, it is essential to have in mind at all times what the function of written pleadings is. Remember that the principal function of pleadings is to explain what a party's case is about, both to the party's opponent and to the court.[9] For a pursuer, this means that the initial writ or summons should make clear what they want (the remedy), why they want it (the facts) and why they should get it (the pleas-in-law). Defences, or answers, should make clear why the pursuer should not get what they want, either in fact or in law, or both; and in addition, set out any additional defences which might be available, such as no jurisdiction or prescription. At the same time, each party's written pleadings should give fair notice to the other of what their case is.

In other words, the precise issues of fact and law which the court has to decide should be readily apparent from a reading

---

[8] 2nd edn, T A Fyfe (1920).

[9] *JD v Lothian Health Board* [2017] CSIH 27, 2018 SCLR 1 at para 32 per Lord Brodie. See also Lees (ibid).

of both (or all) parties' pleadings. Not only should the pleadings make those issues obvious, but they will inform the court's
decision as to what procedure should most appropriately be
adopted in order to resolve the case and as to what documents
may be recovered. As Lees put it, in a passage which still holds
good today:

> The object of the written pleading is to elicit what are the mat-
> ters essential to the decision of the cause, on which parties are
> agreed, or as to which they differ ... The points on which they
> differ are the issue, and matters which are said to be 'put in
> issue' are the material points which must be determined in
> order that the case may be decided.[10]

Too often, even in the Court of Session, and even with pleadings which are not as bad as those criticised by Sheriff Principal
Anwar and Lady Dorrian, it can be difficult to work out after
laboriously reading page after page of voluminous pleadings
what the issues are.[11]

We acknowledge that there can be a tension between the
need for concise pleadings on the one hand, and the requirement to give fair notice on the other. The skilful pleader knows
where to draw the line between brevity and prolixity. The cardinal rule is to think about the legal issues before you set pen
to paper (metaphorically or otherwise). Remember the maxim:
sometimes less is more. Avoid 'Stream of Consciousness
Pleading'. Or, as Lady Dorrian put it: analyse the circumstances of the case in terms which clearly specify the alleged
legal consequences said to arise out of the facts and the legal
duties which follow, and specify clearly the remedies sought
and their basis. Follow that advice and you cannot go far
wrong, whatever the nature of the case you are pleading.

---

[10] Lees, p 1.
[11] In commercial actions, and judicial reviews, the court will often
    require parties to lodge statements of issues of fact and law. Argu-
    ably, the issues should be evident from properly drafted pleadings
    rendering further statements of issues unnecessary.

Finally, we should acknowledge the metaphorical elephant in the room: the Rules rewrite project currently being undertaken by the Scottish Civil Justice Council which will eventually result in a radical new approach to civil procedure in the Court of Session and sheriff court, including the abolition of the distinction between summons and petition procedure and a deliberate 'move away from traditional pleadings where the content was largely left to the parties to determine'.[12] Insofar as written pleadings are concerned, we are likely to see a drive towards simpler phraseology and official discouragement of at least some of the stock phrases currently in use, as well as a cap on the number of words which may be used.

Glossary of useful terms

Written pleadings	Together, the statements made by parties of their respective cases.
Initial writ/ summons/petition	The pursuer's or petitioner's written pleading in the sheriff court/Court of Session, as the case may be.
Defences/answers	The defender's (or respondent's) written pleading.
Craves/conclusions	That part of the initial writ or summons which sets out the remedy or remedies sought; always appearing at the beginning.
Condescendence	That part of the initial writ or summons which sets out the facts relied upon by the pursuer. Divided into numbered paragraphs, known as **articles of condescendence**.
Pleas-in-law	The propositions of law relied upon.
Adjustment	The process by which the written pleadings are altered as of right.
Amendment	The process by which the written pleadings may be altered with leave of the court.

---

[12] The Scottish Civil Justice Council, "The New Civil Procedure Rules – Second Report", para. 2.5.

Petition	The initiating document in applications to the Court of Session which must be made by way of petition, such as a petition for judicial review, or statutory applications.
Prayer	A communication with your deity which may be necessary when appearing in court with poor pleadings; or that part of the petition which sets out the remedies sought; confusingly appearing at the end.
Summary application	The initiating document in statutory/certain common law applications to the sheriff court (which confusingly may also be referred to as an initial writ).
Admitted	The term used when admitting that a specific averment made by an opposing averment is accepted to be true.
Not known and not admitted	The term used when an averment is not denied but is not necessarily accepted to be true.
Denied	(Self-explanatory.)
Believed to be true	The phrase used in pleadings to indicate that an averment is not known to be true but is accepted as true to narrow the issues.
Quoad ultra	'Everything else'.
Separatim	'Separately'.
Esto	Often misused but literally: 'If it be the case that'.
Brevitatis causa	'For the sake of brevity'.
Explained and averred	An arguably unnecessary phrase often used to introduce averments containing an explanation.[13]

---

[13] Akin to opening a letter with the words 'I am writing…' – what else could you be doing?

CHAPTER TWO

Drafting the Writ

A 'writ' is a document containing the written pleadings in court proceedings and it is normally used to refer to the document initiating those proceedings. The precise name given to the initiating writ varies, not only depending on the court in which the proceedings are commenced, but also on the particular type of proceedings raised. In the sheriff court, for example, a 'claim form' initiates a simple procedure action while summary causes are commenced by a 'summons'; ordinary actions – which include most commercial, family and personal injury proceedings – are commenced by an 'initial writ'; bankruptcy proceedings by a 'petition for sequestration'; and summary applications, somewhat counterintuitively, are also commenced by initial writ.[1] Matters are more straightforward in the Court of Session where all actions – i.e. proceedings between two or more parties seeking to enforce or protect an existing legal right – are commenced by a summons; and in situations where the administrative jurisdiction of the court is needed to achieve something where no legal right currently exists, proceedings are commenced by a petition.[2]

---

[1] For a detailed, and up-to-date, treatment of the different types of procedure in the sheriff court, see Macphail, *Sheriff Court Practice*.

[2] See The Hon Lord Carloway, "Civil Procedure", in *The Laws of Scotland: Stair Memorial Encyclopaedia*, Reissue (2007) para 87; and ch 6. But this distinction is likely soon to be abolished, when the rules rewrite project being undertaken by the Scottish Civil Justice Council comes to fruition: see p 7.

For present purposes, do not worry about the terminology. While the focus of this chapter is on how to draft the most common type of writ, namely the initial writ/the summons, we are concerned in the first place with the work you need to do before any drafting work, of any description, is done at all. The suggestions made in the pages to follow apply with the same force regardless of the type of case or the court in which it is raised.

Analysing your case

Before you power-up your computer and begin typing, there is one very important thing you should always do – and that is you should *think*. Think about what your client's problem actually is and whether there is a solution. Think what it is that you want the court to do for your client and what legal hurdles require to be surmounted before the court can do it. You must never ever begin to draft a writ until you are clear in your own mind what your case is about. This process is known as the case analysis.

There is no one-size-fits-all approach to conducting your case analysis. It will depend on the nature of the instruction, how it is to be funded, the urgency of the matter and the time and resources that you have at your disposal. What is offered here are some thoughts, we hope of broad applicability.

What's the story?

This might seem obvious, but it is essential that you under-stand what has prompted your client to seek legal advice and what it is that they hope you can do to help. It is a big step, for most people, to conclude that the only solution they have left is to consult a solicitor with a view to raising court proceedings. So why have they?

At the very least, you will want to know:

- *What brings the client to your office?* Has something already hap-pened? Are they concerned that something may happen in the future? Are they seeking a remedy for themselves, or on behalf of someone else, for example their child or their company? Ask them to tell their story. You will likely have to go back to this story on many occasions over the course of the litigation, and ideally on several occasions before the writ is drafted. You will need to separate the relevant from the irrelevant and identify the good facts and the bad facts. The story may not be told in a chronological, or even logical, order; it is your job to ask the right questions to facilitate your client telling you exactly what you need to know.

- *What would they like to achieve?* Is it payment of money they say is due to them? Is it a court order to stop something from happening? Is it compensation for an injury they have sustained? Is it a divorce, or the regulation of contact between parents and children? Are they seeking to challenge an administrative decision of a public authority? Whatever it is, you will need to know this up front. Apart from anything else, knowing this at the outset will allow you to advise whether the remedy they seek is something capable, in principle, of being granted by a court or tribunal, and if so, which court or tribunal has the power to grant it.

- *How urgent is the instruction?* It is a good idea to learn by rote the prescription or limitation periods that apply to the most common types of claim. Actions for breach of contract, or payment of a debt, must be raised within five years.[3] In general terms, actions for personal injuries must be raised within three years of the accident.[4] Your client only has one year in which to seek damages for a breach of their human rights,[5] and applications for judicial review must be raised within three months of the issue arising.[6] You must always identify, and identify quickly, the applicable

---

[3] Prescription and Limitation (Scotland) Act 1973 Act, s 6 and Sch 1.
[4] 1973 Act, ss 17-19A.
[5] Human Rights Act 1998, s 7.
[6] Court of Session Act 1988, s 27A.

time-limit.[7] That will tell you, first, whether it is already too late and, if so, whether anything can be done about the lateness; and second, assuming it is not too late, how much time you have left to get proceedings served. Clearly, if your client comes to you seeking an order from the court to stop something due to happen tomorrow, you will have to type very quickly indeed and find a sheriff or judge as soon as humanly possible.[8]

Ideally, the above information from your client will be turned into a precognition. This is a document worth working on carefully. If the process of precognition is done correctly, it will be a document to which you will return throughout the litigation, whether you are acting as solicitor or counsel. It should be the blueprint for drafting the writ, which in turn will be the roadmap for the litigation. Before you actually take the precognition, prepare a list of questions to which you need answers. Do not wing it!

What else do you need?
In addition to the precognition from the client, you will have to give thought to what else you will need to assist with analysing your case and drafting your writ. It should be at the forefront of your mind that you will require to prove the facts that you aver, and that it will be presumed that you will only make an

---

[7] For further reading, see D Johnston, *Prescription and Limitation of Actions*, 2nd edn (2012).

[8] Sheriff courts and the Court of Session will have a rota in place for out-of-hours business. On a particularly memorable occasion, one of our number was instructed on a Saturday afternoon to obtain an *interim* interdict to stop a Sunday newspaper from publishing a story. A (contested) hearing took place before the duty Lord Ordinary in Court 12, Parliament House, in the early hours of the Sunday morning. The motion was refused, and the fact that interdict was sought became part of the story. There may be a lesson there.

averment once satisfied that you will be able to prove it. Lord Brodie reminded pleaders of their duties in *JD v Lothian Health Board*:

> It is not a matter of a party making averments that he would like to be able to prove or hopes he might be able to prove; a party is expected to have prepared his case and that includes finding out from potential witnesses exactly what they are able to say in response to specific questions. It is what potential witnesses say that they will say if required to give evidence that provides the basis of properly made averments. The process of finding out what potential witnesses are able to say is referred to as precognition (foreknowledge). Parties are expected to have precognosced (interviewed) their witnesses in order to find out what they can say; only in exceptional circumstances will it be proper to lead a witness without having previously ascertained exactly what evidence he is able to give. In the case of skilled witnesses the most efficient mechanism for doing that may be to instruct the skilled witness to prepare a report on the issues on which the skilled witness will be asked to give evidence.[9]

Precisely what information you will need will vary depending on the type of case. However, the following questions should be running through your head at the outset of all instructions:

- *What documents do I need?* For example, if your client wishes to pursue an action for damages for breach of contract or an action for specific implement, you will need to see the contract if it is in writing. Has your client emailed you that? If it is a personal injuries action following an accident at work, has your client provided you with any contemporaneous accident report and their GP records? If it is a road traffic accident, do you know precisely where it happened so that you can search for it on Google Maps[10]

---

[9] *JD v Lothian Health Board* [2017] CSIH 27, 2018 SCLR 1 at para 30 per Lord Brodie.

[10] Other electronic maps are available.

and work out how to aver clearly where the accident took place? In an executry matter, having a copy of the will might be a good idea. The title deeds will doubtless assist in a property dispute, and letters, emails or texts showing a debt duly constituted and demands for payment ignored will make life easier if you are instructed to recover a debt. But beware: it is your job to wade through the documents and to determine what relevance, if any, they have to the issues for the court. It is highly inadvisable simply to lodge 249 documents across 17 inventories if you are only going to ask the court to look at 3 of them.

- *Which witnesses should I contact?* A precognition from a potential witness might allow you to add flesh to the bones of your client's story. Did anyone witness the crash? Does someone speak to when, where, by whom and in what terms a verbal contract was entered into? Knowing who will support your client's position – and who will deny seeing anything at all – is essential.

- *Do I need an expert report before I draft the writ?* While a report from a skilled witness may be beneficial if not essential to many litigations, it can be – and sometimes can only be – instructed after the action is raised and defences are lodged.[11] However, there is no such element of choice in medical and other professional negligence actions: it is a matter of professional duty for the solicitor or advocate to have a supportive report from a suitably qualified and

---

[11] Albeit if time permits, and if you have the necessary information, it is always preferable to have the report in-hand before drafting the writ. On when a skilled witness is required and the duties of the 'expert' witness generally, see *Kennedy v Cordia (Services) LLP* [2016] UKSC 6, 2016 SC (UKSC) 59.

experienced expert *before* it is averred that a professional person was negligent.[12]

- *Who is the defender?* What is the defender's name (it is particularly important to get this right when suing a company)? Should there be just one defender or should there be multiple defenders? In what capacity is the defender to be sued? Where is the defender based? There may be situations where you and your client simply do not know who should be sued. While all attempts to resolve that issue should be made before the writ is drafted, you may require to sue multiple parties in the first instance, and to be prepared to let some of them out of the action in due course – and to accept the expenses consequences that will inevitably follow.

If you follow the above, you should be in possession of the facts (or at least the facts as told to you). You will have been supplied with any necessary supporting documentation. You will hopefully have statements from potential witnesses. You may even have an expert report.

Your job then is to analyse this information and decide upon the nature of your client's claim and the legal grounds upon which that claim is based. If you know what the applicable law is, you should not have too much difficulty in deciding what has to be incorporated into the initiating writ. If you are not sure of the legal nature of your client's claim, or if you do not know what the law is on the point, then you will not have a clue what is essential and what is not. You then may be confronted with the temptation to shove into your writ everything

---

[12] *JD v Lothian Health Board* (n 9) at para 54 per Lady Clark of Calton. The report must deal with the test for professional negligence as set out in *Hunter v Hanley* 1954 SC 200 at 204 per the Lord President (Clyde). For a judicial challenge to this received wisdom, see *Cockburn v Hope* [2024] CSOH 69 at paras 18–25 per Lord Sandison. See also Chapter 6.

you can think of in the way of remedies, facts and pleas in the hope (often forlorn) that somewhere in the jumble there is something that will stick. But remember what Lord Brodie said in *JD*. If you prefer 19th-century *dicta*, have a look at what Lord President McNeill said in 1856:

> I do not understand how anyone can frame a record properly without having in his mind the issue he wishes to try, and selecting from the materials before him those, and those only, that are pertinent to that issue. To throw into a record all matters directly or indirectly connected with the case, or having any possible bearing on it, is not the right way of framing a record; it may save the trouble of thinking at that stage, and relieve from the labour of selecting and arranging the materials; but it is not the right way of framing a record, and it multiplies the subsequent labour and risks of miscarriage, and adds greatly to the expense. A party should, while preparing a record, have the issue he wishes to try steadily in view, and direct his materials to that end.[13]

So always, before you start drafting, think what it is that your client wants and the legal ground or grounds on which they are entitled to get it. If you are not clear in your own mind what the legal basis of your client's case is, your writ will suffer, perhaps fatally. If your client wants money, you must decide what that money represents – is it a debt owed to him for goods supplied or services performed? Is it damages and, if so, are the damages contractual or delictual? Or is your client simply wanting their money back because goods they have bought have turned out to be useless or defective? Is there a statutory case of fault? What is the potential value of the claim? Which court can (or must) the action be raised in? Is it an application for judicial review or, properly analysed, is it simply an action

---

[13] *Anderson v Glasgow and South-Western Railway Co* (1865) 4 M 259 at 261 per the Lord President (McNeil).

for damages?[14] Or is it something which can only be resolved by a tribunal?[15]

Always slot your client's claim into its appropriate legal pigeonhole and refresh your memory about what the law is on the point in question. Look up the appropriate textbooks. When those textbooks cite cases as authority for a proposition, look up those cases on Westlaw[16] to make sure that they say what the textbook says that they say and that they remain good law. Go through the pain barrier of investigating the facts, researching the law and applying the law to those facts.

Having done that, it will hopefully be clearer what matters your writ will require to cover. Continue to subject your initial analysis to anxious scrutiny. Face up to the negative aspects of your client's case: they may not be insurmountable obstacles, but if they are, then early, frank advice is always the best strategy. Your client will never thank you for wasting their time (and/or their money) on a hopeless cause.

Finally, having decided what form of action to raise, you will need to consider whether the subject matter is governed by

---

[14] In answering that question, try to avoid getting as stuck as the Inner House did in *Ruddy v Chief Constable of Strathclyde Police* [2012] UKSC 57, 2013 SC (UKSC) 126. In that regard, you should find out if your office has a copy of L Drummond, F McCartney and A Poole, *A Practical Guide to Public Law Litigation in Scotland* (2020) and ask your boss to purchase it if it doesn't.

[15] Tribunals are beyond the scope of this book but you should familiarise yourself with the situations in which a dispute requires to be initiated in any of the chambers of the First-tier Tribunal, the Mental Health Tribunal, the Employment Tribunal, the Lands Tribunal for Scotland and so on. Likewise, this book is not concerned with the Scottish Land Court or Children's Hearings, and, regrettably, we did not have time to deal with the Court of the Lord Lyon.

[16] Other legal databases are available.

a pre-action protocol requiring correspondence before court proceedings are raised.[17]

Jurisdiction and competence

Before considering the constituent parts of an initial writ (which consideration will apply equally to a summons, leaving matters of nomenclature to the side), it is necessary to say something about jurisdiction and exclusive competence. These are not straightforward matters and a good working knowledge of the Court of Session and sheriff court rules, together with the Civil Jurisdiction and Judgments Act 1982 and the Courts Reform (Scotland) Act 2014, is essential. Macphail's *Sheriff Court Practice* is an excellent place to start. But for now, the following should get you thinking along the right lines:

- The sheriff court has exclusive jurisdiction for claims below a total aggregate value of £100,000, exclusive of interest and expenses.[18] In other words, claims under that value cannot be raised in the Court of Session.[19] There is, however, no upper limit on the value of claims which can be raised in the sheriff court, and the sheriff court and the Court of Session have concurrent jurisdiction to hear claims worth over £100,000. It should go without saying that the Court of Session can hear cases stemming from any part of Scotland.
- The Court of Session has exclusive jurisdiction in relation to certain proceedings concerned with personal status, such as reduction of decrees of divorce. Only the Court of Session can reduce a decree of another court or suspend

---

[17] See Chapter 5.

[18] Courts Reform (Scotland) Act 2014, s 39. That rule does not apply to family proceedings unless the only order sought is for aliment.

[19] But they can be remitted: see Courts Reform (Scotland) Act 2014, s 92.

a charge proceeding upon a Court of Session decree. If you are instructed in a matter concerning a trust, think Court of Session – as you should if instructed in relation to the winding-up of a company.[20] Only the Court of Session can deal with judicial reviews, and don't even contemplate asking a sheriff to hear a petition to the *nobile officium* or to exercise a *parens patriae* jurisdiction.[21]

- The general rule is that the sheriff court in the place where the defender is domiciled has jurisdiction. In broad terms, that means the court in the place where the defender lives or is based. So if the person who owes your client money lives in Charlotte Square, Edinburgh, then Edinburgh Sheriff Court has jurisdiction. In actions based on contract, the court in the place of contractual performance also has jurisdiction. Likewise, in delictual actions, the court for the place where the harmful event occurred has jurisdiction too. So if the hot-shot Texan oil executive is on a business trip to Pennan, Aberdeenshire, and while there crashes his car into your client's car as she is approaching her driveway – suddenly and without warning, of course – then proceedings against him can be raised at your client's local court, in that case Banff Sheriff Court.[22] Companies can be sued at the place of their registered office or in the court in a place in which they do business. The sheriff court in the place where property is situated usually has jurisdiction to determine rights of ownership or possession. Note that special rules exist to assist consumers in consumer contract disputes. It is also worth remembering that the Crown – including the Scottish Ministers and the

[20] Unless the company has a share capital of less than £120,000, in which case, the action should be raised in the sheriff court (see: Insolvency Act 1986, s 120(3)).
[21] Macphail, *Sheriff Court Practice* is excellent on all of this: see ch 2.
[22] Or in the All Scotland Personal Injury Court – see Chapter 6.

Lord Advocate – are domiciled throughout the country.[23] If you are doubtful about which sheriffdom or which sheriff court within the sheriffdom has jurisdiction, look up the Scottish Courts and Tribunals Service's website which has a 'Gazetteer' into which you can plug in the name of a town and be rewarded with the name of the sheriff court which has jurisdiction.[24]

- Claims in the sheriff court worth more than £5,000 are governed by the ordinary procedure rules. If the claim is worth no more than £5,000, it requires to be raised under the simple procedure[25] (with the exception of personal injury actions under £5,000 and certain other actions[26]).

- As a result of the Courts Reform (Scotland) Act 2014, a sheriff may grant an interdict that has effect in relation to conduct both within and outwith their sheriffdom, so long as the court otherwise has jurisdiction to hear the action.[27]

- Actions arising from personal injuries or death that occurred anywhere in Scotland can be raised in the Sheriff Personal Injury Court based at Edinburgh Sheriff Court, which has a Scotland-wide jurisdiction and is commonly referred to as 'ASSPIC' (an acronym for the misnomer:

---

[23] For all of this, see the Civil Jurisdiction and Judgments Act 1982, in particular Sch. 8. See also Macphail, *Sheriff Court Practice*, ch 3; in particular for the exceptions.

[24] Available at https://scotcourts.gov.uk/the-courts/gazetteer.

[25] Courts Reform (Scotland) Act 2014, s 72.

[26] For example, certain heritable actions are raised as summary cause actions (or otherwise in the First-tier Tribunal (Housing and Property Chamber)). Summary cause actions are governed by the Summary Cause Rules 2002. It is understood that in the fullness of time, such claims will be transferred to the simple procedure.

[27] 2014 Act, s 84.

the 'All-Scotland Sheriff Personal Injury Court').[28] Note that its jurisdiction is concurrent, not exclusive: a pursuer may still elect to raise such proceedings in their local sheriff court.[29]

Finally, it is worth remembering that questions of jurisdiction and competence are *pars judicis*; that is, it is the duty of the court to be satisfied that it can competently hear a cause brought before it and to decline to hear it if it does not. Indeed, you may not even get that far: the sheriff clerk may decline to warrant the writ. But assuming you have identified correctly which court you can or must raise your action in, and that you have complied with any pre-action protocol, it is time to come on to the drafting.

The drafting

The function of the initial writ is to set out what you want, whom you want it from and why you should get it. If you are not sure what you want, whom you want it from or why you should get it, then you should ask yourself seriously (before someone else, like the sheriff, does) what you are doing raising an action at all.

---

[28] Courts Reform (Scotland) Act 2014, s 42. See the All-Scotland Sheriff Court (Sheriff Personal Injury Court) Order 2015 (SSI 2015/213) for its jurisdiction; it is worth noting that actions worth between £1,000 and £5,000 can be raised in 'ASSPIC' if they relate to work-place accidents or if transferred there by a sheriff.

[29] If you are a solicitor in Aberdeen, acting for an Aberdonian who lives in Aberdeen, and if the accident occurred in Aberdeen, and if all or most of the witnesses live in Aberdeen, you would have to wonder whether there would be any benefit in raising the action anywhere other than in Aberdeen. Aside from that court's expertise, one such benefit may be the availability of the civil jury trial in ASSPIC but not in other sheriff courts: Courts Reform (Scotland) Act 2014, s 63.

But getting the pleadings right is not just about conforming to some abstract rules or nodding to custom. It is about recognising that the pleadings are as much an exercise in advocacy as is making a submission in court. As Lord President Carloway said in a talk to practitioners:

> The court has specific expectations about the form and content of written pleadings … The written pleadings give the first instance judge the first – and often abiding – impression of the case and its prospects. They provide the first opportunity to persuade the judge of the strength of the case. The pleadings should be directed towards assisting the court to come to a correct view of the case, rather than hindering it from doing so. Written pleadings should, above all, be concise and readable, but sufficiently detailed to give the judge a clear steer towards what the case is about. There is an unexpected problem at the moment, even in commercial procedure, of pleadings being so lengthy, convoluted and diffuse as to serve only to obscure the matters for determination.[30]

And with that in mind, it is time to consider the writ.

The writ is divided into six parts:

(a)   The heading (which court?)
(b)   The description (what is this document?)
(c)   The instance (who?)
(d)   The crave (what remedy?)[31]
(e)   The condescendence (who did what to whom and where, when and how was it done?)[32]

---

[30] The Rt Hon Lord Carloway, "How To Win Your Case: What the Court Expects from Advocates", Talk at the Faculty of Advocates to mark International Women's Day, 8 March 2018 (available here: https://www.advocates.org.uk/media/2727/iwd18carloway.pdf).
[31] Known as the conclusion in a Court of Session summons.
[32] Known as the statement of claim in a personal injuries action and the statement of facts in a petition.

(f) The pleas-in-law (why should the court grant the remedy?)[33]

The writ is structured so that the pleas-in-law connect the facts averred in the condescendence to the remedy sought in the crave.[34] Each of these six parts is now considered.[35]

(a) **The heading**

Here you simply state which sheriffdom and district the action is being raised in. There may be only one sheriff court which has jurisdiction over the defender. If so, then obviously the action has to be raised there (unless you decide to go for a Court of Session action instead). If more than one sheriff court has, or could have, jurisdiction, then you may wish to raise the action in whichever court is most convenient for you, your client and your witnesses (or, possibly, in ASSPIC, even if geographically inconvenient, to obtain the benefit of that court's expertise).

Be sure you get the heading right. Say 'Sheriffdom of Tayside, Central and Fife at Falkirk' and not merely 'Sheriff Court, Falkirk'. And remember that the title of the most northerly sheriffdom is 'Grampian, Highland [without an "s"] and Islands [with an "s"]', and that the title of the sheriffdom which includes Edinburgh is 'Sheriffdom of Lothian [not "the Lothians"] and Borders'. If you are raising an action in ASSPIC, you head the writ 'Sheriffdom of Lothian and Borders at Edinburgh in the All-Scotland Sheriff Court'.

---

[33] Petitions in the Court of Session have 'prayers' rather than pleas-in-law; unless it is a petition for judicial review, which has pleas-in-law.

[34] W A Wilson, *Introductory Essays on Scots Law*, 2nd edn (1984), p 64.

[35] You should have regard to the rules of court (both sheriff court and Court of Session) and to the appended forms for precisely what is required of the initiating writ in the different procedures.

A Court of Session summons is headed 'In the Court of Session'.

(b) The description
This comes directly below the heading and tells the reader what document they are looking at. If you are drafting an initial writ, the description 'INITIAL WRIT' should appear. The same goes if it is a 'SUMMONS'. If it is a writ drafted pursuant to a particular procedure, that procedure should be identified in the description, for example 'INITIAL WRIT (personal injuries action/commercial action)'.

After the description but before the instance, you should insert '*in causa*' or 'in the cause'.

(c) The instance
This is where you identify the parties.[36] The primary purpose of it is to identify the parties sufficiently for the purposes of citation and the execution of diligence. Normally, you will not have any difficulty in deciding who the pursuer should be: it is likely to be the man who has spent the day in your office and followed up with emails attaching emails embedded with yet further attachments. But is the claim really his, or should the pursuer be his company, a trading name, his child, the relative over whom he has a power of attorney, the partnership of which he is a member or the golf club of which he is captain? Or should the pursuer be his wife who is the one who actually owns the villa in Barnton that the neighbour's wind turbine fell on top of and destroyed?

Once you have decided that your client is the proper pursuer, give him his full name and his address – not an

---

[36] For a full discussion of parties and questions of capacity, title and interest, see Macphail, *Sheriff Court Practice*, ch 4.

accommodation address such as 'care of' your office.[37] If it is your client's home address, the words 'residing at' should be used before the address itself. If the pursuer is suing in a particular capacity, such as executor-nominate or trust, that must be made clear in the instance. If the pursuer is in receipt of legal aid, the words 'Assisted Person' must appear in brackets following their name.

Deciding who the proper defender is can often be considerably more difficult. Is it a natural person or a company? If your instructions are to sue an individual, then matters are likely to be more straightforward and you will simply need to find out their full name and home address. But it may be a natural person acting in a particular capacity, such as trustee, executor or partner in a firm. Remember that it is a very different thing to raise an action against 'Jimmy Snooks' as opposed to 'Jimmy Snooks, as guardian of Janey Snooks' or to raise an action against 'Dorothy Bain' rather than against 'The Rt Hon. Dorothy Bain KC, His Majesty's Advocate'. If it is a company or a limited liability partnership, you will need to find out its registered office or a place of its business and its company or partnership number. Companies in the same group with names which are almost identical can cause particular problems.[38] If your client wishes to sue his employer, remember that his wage slip may be positively misleading, e.g. 'University of Edinburgh', where the correct defender is 'The

---

[37] On this, and on principles of open justice generally, see *MH v Mental Health Tribunal for Scotland* [2019] CSIH 14, 2019 SC 432. It is, however, generally acceptable to design prisoners, e.g. as 'John Smith, at present a prisoner in HM Prison Barlinnie'. See also what is said in Chapter 5 on how to deal with anonymisation in particularly sensitive cases; and also Macphail, *Sheriff Court Practice*, ch 9 on this and on withholding addresses.

[38] See, for example, *Perth and Kinross Council v Scottish Water Ltd* [2016] CSIH 83, 2017 SC 164.

University Court of the University of Edinburgh'.[39] If it is the government, you will need to know if it is the UK or Scottish government. Particularly in Scotland, beware of the government departments and agencies that do not have legal personality. For example, if your client wishes to sue the Scottish Prison Service, the correct defender is 'The Scottish Ministers, Victoria Quay, Edinburgh EH6 6QQ'.[40]

If you have got time, write and ask the would-be defender what its proper name is or which company within a group of companies actually employed your client. Clicking on the 'About us' page of a company or public authority's website can often shed some light, as can a search on the Companies House website.[41] And as with the pursuer, so with the defender; give the full address of their residence or place of business.

Be careful about raising actions in the name of a plurality of pursuers or against a plurality of defenders. It is competent for two or more pursuers to join in one action against the same defender if they have a connection with one another in the

---

[39] In this regard, *Green's Litigation Styles* (Looseleaf, and updated regularly electronically and on CD-ROM) is exceedingly useful for finding example instances for nearly every-conceivable company, partnership, public authority, unincorporated association and so on.

[40] It is probably the case that actions against the Scottish Ministers should be raised against the Lord Advocate on behalf of the Ministers (see J L Jamieson, "Devolution and the Scottish Law Officers", 1999 SLT (News) 121), but this is rarely if ever done. If in doubt as to who to sue in matters of government/the Crown, particularly as between the Lord Advocate and the Advocate General for Scotland, assistance can be found in the Crown Suits (Scotland) Act 1857, the Crown Proceedings Act 1947, the Scotland Act 1998, s 126 (specifically the definition of 'Scottish Administration') and the associated Scottish Administration (Offices) Order 1999 SI 1999/1127.

[41] https://www.gov.uk/government/organisations/companies -house.

matter pursued for or have been aggrieved by the same act.[42] But two pursuers cannot conjoin in one action in respect of separate and independent wrongs.[43] Where a number of pursuers are injured in the same accident, it is usually competent for all to sue in the one action provided that the grounds of action are identical and that there is no material prejudice to the defender.[44] Where various members of a family are claiming under the Damages (Scotland) Act 2011 in respect of the death of a relative, all entitled pursuers must combine in the same action.[45]

It is incompetent for a pursuer to seek a decree against multiple defenders on separate and unconnected grounds inferring separate individual liability,[46] and it is not competent to seek to have two or more defenders found liable, on a joint and several basis, for separate causes of action.[47] But a pursuer can convene multiple defenders in a single action if they have all combined to cause the same damage to the pursuer (e.g. joint

[42] *Feuars of Orkney v Steuart* (1741) M 11986.

[43] Summarised by the Lord President (Hope) in *Boulting v Elias* 1990 SC 135. See also *Prosper Properties Ltd v Scottish Ministers* 2012 CSOH 136 at para 18 per Lord Woolman.

[44] *Buchan v Thomson* 1976 SLT 42 at 44. Related but different is the relatively new concept of 'group proceedings' (the Scottish answer to 'class actions') introduced by the Civil Litigation (Expenses and Group Proceedings) (Scotland) Act 2018, s 20 and governed by RCS, ch 26A. For a summary of the procedure see *Bridgehouse v Bayerische Motoren Werke Aktiengesellschaft* [2024] CSOH 2, 2024 SLT 116 at paras 4 to 17 per Lord Ericht.

[45] See p 82.

[46] *Liquidators of the Western Bank of Scotland v Douglas* (1860) 22 D 446 at 497 per the Lord Justice Clerk (Inglis). See also *Ellerman Lined Ltd v Clyde Navigations Trs* 1909 SC 690 at 691–692 per the Lord President (Dunedin).

[47] *Barr v Neilson* (1868) 6 M. 651. See Macphail, *Sheriff Court Practice*, ch 4 at paras 4.48 *et seq* for guidance on joint, and joint and several liability.

and several liability in delict) or if they are all liable to him jointly and severally where different breaches of contract have produced a common result.[48] That is permissible because it is viewed as a single wrong. But the court may permit actions to proceed against multiple defenders, on separate grounds, where considerations of convenience favour letting it proceed to proof as a whole because the cases are factually and legally linked.[49] In that situation the litmus test for determining if the action is incompetent is whether, as framed, it is likely to lead to manifest inconvenience and injustice.[50]

(d) The crave

This is where you set out what it is that you want the court to do for your client. The decree of the court, if you are success-ful at the end of the day, will normally follow the crave of the writ closely (if not exactly), so it is important that you should get it right.

You will find styles of craves (actually conclusions, but you should not have any trouble adapting them) appended to form 13.2-B to the Rules of the Court of Session.[51] Further styles can be found in *Green's Litigation Styles*. Your office will prob-ably also have its own style bank. If it does not, you should start one yourself. Once so armed, select the form of crave as relevant to your type of action, remembering always to modify any relevant parts – the actual sum sued for in particular! But be intelligent and discriminating about it. Remember that the law may have changed since the date the style was drafted (e.g. as regards rates of interest and the date from which interest can

---

[48] *Grunwald v Hughes* 1965 SLT 209.
[49] *Toner v Kean Construction (Scotland) Ltd* [2009] CSOH 105, 2009 SLT 1038.
[50] *Ruddy v Chief Constable of Strathclyde Police* (n 14) at para 32 per Lord Hope of Craighead.
[51] Available here: https://scotcourts.gov.uk/rules-and-practice/forms/court-of-session-forms.

be claimed; the grounds of separation and divorce; the entities responsible for matters post-devolution). There should be one crave for each remedy sought. If the action is one for payment (whether of damages or of a debt) and there is more than one defender, remember to specify whether their liability is joint, or joint and several. Remember that it is also competent to crave decree for payment in a currency other than sterling. Above all else, try to frame the crave so that an interlocutor giving you the decree that you want can be drafted by reference to the precise terms of the crave. Making life easier for the sheriff or judge (or their clerk!) is never a wasted endeavour.

The only craves you are likely to have any difficulty in drafting are the ones you will need to make up yourself from scratch, such as declarators, interdicts and craves for specific implement.

Here are some hints relating to the drafting of craves which are not in standard form and have to be tailor-made for each occasion:

1. Don't be vague: spell out what you want in detail. If you want a declarator that your client owns a particular piece of heritable property, then your crave should contain the full conveyancing description of the ground. Don't simply cross-refer to the description contained in a disposition executed and recorded on a particular date. You want a decree which can be understood and read by itself; not one which means nothing unless read along with some other document.[52] If you are seeking declarator that your client and the defender entered into an oral contract, you should specify in the crave the date upon which they did so

---

[52] In some situations it is permissible, even necessary, to refer to another document, for example when seeking interdict against infringement of copyright in artistic works, where you may annex the works in question to the summons (in turn, if an order is granted, they will require to be annexed to the court's interlocutor).

and all of its essential terms. A crave for declarator which is ambiguous or imprecise is incompetent.[53] Vagueness is especially to be avoided when you are seeking specific implement. You cannot simply ask the court to ordain the defender to implement the contract entered into between him and the pursuer on a particular date.[54] You must set out in words of preferably one syllable just what it is that the defender will have to do to implement the contract, how he should do it and the time (which should be a reasonable time) within which he has got to do it. Remember that the court will generally decline to entertain an application for declarator of a hypothetical or academic question.[55] Similarly, craves for interdict should be drafted with great precision.[56] While you may be allowed to amend to put matters right if there is any ambiguity or vagueness, you may not succeed in getting *interim* interdict there and then (and getting *interim* interdict is very often the whole

---

[53] See *Rothfield v North British Railway Company* 1920 SC 805 where the declarator sought was 'much too vague and general' and 'crowded with words phrases and words of quite indefinite meaning': at 838 per Lord Ormidale.

[54] *Robertson v Cockburn* (1875) 3 R 21. See also *Retail Parks Investments Ltd v The Royal Bank of Scotland plc* 1996 SC 227.

[55] For extensive discussion of this, see *Wightman v Secretary of State for Exiting the European Union* [2018] CSIH 62, 2019 SC at para 21 *et seq* per the Lord President (Carloway); and *Keatings v Advocate General for Scotland* [2021] CSIH 25, 2021 SC 329 at para 51 *et seq* per the Lord President (Carloway).

[56] In *Jepuson UK Ltd v E&A International Ltd* [2024] SC EDIN 35, Sheriff Campbell KC was unwilling to interpret an interdict prohibiting the defender from producing a type of bag with Harris Tweed as a prohibition against its producing 'any similarly patterned woollen cloth'.

point of the exercise).[57] In any event, it is unwise – at any stage of an action – to proceed on the assumption that the court will allow the pleadings to be amended (or make any discretionary and thus virtually unappealable decision in your client's favour!).[58]

2. Don't be greedy: don't draft your crave in such a way as to try to obtain more than your client is legally entitled to. (We're not talking here about craves for payment of damages, in which the practice since time immemorial, though certainly not endorsed, is to sue for about twice what you hope eventually to get.) If you are seeking interdict against breach of a term of a contract by the defender (e.g. a covenant against competition) your crave should follow strictly the terms of the contract with all its qualifications and exceptions, including time-limits and territorial limitations. Do not try to paraphrase it – you are bound to make it too wide (or too narrow, which is just as bad from your client's point of view). Once you have set out in the crave the exact terms of the obligation, breach of which you want to have interdicted, by all means, if you wish, go on to incorporate specific prohibitions. You may know, for example, that a former employee who is subject to a covenant against soliciting the pursuer's customers has been approaching some particular customers. There is no harm in such a case, after you have craved interdict in the precise terms of the covenant, from going on to say 'and, in particular, but without prejudice to the foregoing

---

[57] On interdicts – both perpetual and *ad interim* – H Burn-Murdoch, *Interdict in the Law of Scotland* (1933) remains a valuable resource. It is also important to bear in mind the availability of various statutory interdicts, e.g. under the Protection from Harassment Act 1997 or the Protection from Abuse (Scotland) Act 2001, and any crave seeking such an interdict must refer to the statutory provision under which it is sought.

[58] Amendments are dealt with in Chapter 4.

generality, to grant decree interdicting the defender for X period from soliciting orders from the following customers of the pursuers...'. Another reason for not being greedy (and this applies to craves for payment of debts or damages as well as to craves for interdict, declarator or specific implement) is that if you stick strictly to claiming what you are entitled to and no more, there is a greater chance that the action will not be defended.

3. Don't forget that you may not get what you are principally asking for. But that does not necessarily mean that you will not get anything at all. So think what your fall-back position is and insert an alternative crave for that. You may want specific implement. But there can be any number of reasons why the court might refuse to grant it even though your client is in the right. So you should have an alternative crave for damages, failing decree of implement. Similarly, if you are seeking delivery of an item of corporeal moveable property, you should have an alternative crave for damages, failing delivery. You can also have ancillary or eventual craves. In actions raised under the Human Rights Act 1998, it is normal to have an eventual crave. The first crave should be for declarator that the defender public authority acted incompatibly with a relevant Article of the European Convention on Human Rights and thus unlawfully in terms of section 6 of the 1998 Act; and the second crave should seek damages as "just satisfaction" for the violation. While in reality your client may only care about obtaining damages, you must crave the declarator too, since the court may decide that declarator alone will provide "just satisfaction".[59]

4. Don't forget that you cannot get what you have not asked for. For example, if you want *interim* interdict, you should

---

[59] Human Rights Act 1998, s 8.

ask for it in the crave.[60] If you want a warrant for arrestment to found jurisdiction or a warrant to arrest or inhibit on the dependence be sure to ask for it.[61] And of course, you always seek expenses.[62] On craves for payment, you always ask for interest. Give careful thought to the rate of interest and the date from which interest should run.[63] Remember that the parties may have expressly agreed to a higher rate of interest than the judicial rate. And don't forget to give thought to whether separate craves should be directed against different defenders, if you are suing more than one.

(e) The condescendence

The structure

This is where you set out the facts and your grounds of action. This you should do in short, numbered paragraphs. Within those short paragraphs you should avoid all argument and you should write in short sentences unencumbered, as far as possible, with adjectives, adverbs and subordinate clauses. Keep it simple. Avoid vituperative verbiage. As Lord Carloway said:

---

[60] Craving separately for interdict *ad interim* is not, in fact, strictly necessary, so long as perpetual interdict is craved (see *National Cash Register v Kinnear* 1948 SLT (Notes) 83), but it is almost always done.

[61] Diligence on the dependence has been described by the UK Supreme Court as a 'draconian remedy' (*Anwar v Advocate General for Scotland* [2021] UKSC 44, 2021 SLT 1453 at para 58 per Lord Hodge). Be sure to familiarise yourself with the Debtors (Scotland) Act 1987 as amended by the Bankruptcy and Diligence etc. (Scotland) Act 2007.

[62] Again, not technically necessary but always done, and of potentially critical importance should the action be undefended.

[63] For assistance, see Macphail, *Sheriff Court Practice*, ch 9 and paras 9.101–9.102. It's also wise to remember the circumstances in which the pursuer can reap the benefits of the Late Payment of Commercial Debts (Interest) Act 1998.

One of the central skills which the advocate must develop is the effective distillation of complex ideas into simple, concise language. This skill is particularly required in written pleadings. Counsel should use modern, plain English in both written pleadings and oral submissions. The accuracy and clarity of the language, which is used to express ideas, are undoubtedly what will ultimately impress the court and may be decisive in a narrow case. Some judges have, in the past, made life difficult for the economic pleader, but I would have hoped that we have put those days firmly behind us.[64]

With that in mind, there are two essential functions which every condescendence must fulfil:

1. It must state facts which, if true, are such as to justify, or entitle the pursuer to, decree in terms of his crave: **the 'relevancy' essential**.

2. It must give fair notice to the defender of the case which he has to meet: **the 'fair notice' essential**. Lord President Clyde expressed the matter thus:

> The object of a condescendence is not merely to give fair notice to the other side of what the framer hopes to establish in fact, but—coupled with the … Pleas-in-Law—to present a relevant case, that is, to disclose a position in fact and law which requires or justifies the remedy asked.

---

[64] "How To Win Your Case: What the Court Expects from Advocates" (n 30). Thanks to the industry of David Parratt KC, we now know that a lack of concision is not a new complaint of judges. Indeed, by Article of Regulation recorded in the Sederunt Book of 1695, the Court of Session could impose a fine on counsel who drafted pleadings which were 'groundless, or in [their] length superfluous or litigious', D R Parratt, *The Development and Use of Written Pleadings in Scots Civil Procedure*, PhD Thesis (2004), at 68. We are not aware of any current proposals to reinstate that power.

> It is as if the pursuer came into court and said: 'This is a summary of my case.' The summary must be sufficiently full to enable the court to determine whether, assuming the facts to be verified either (a) instanter by admission or by probative documents or (b) by evidence to be subsequently led, the pursuer has a good case in law. If the pursuer fails in this, his case is dismissed without inquiry into the matters of fact alleged on either side. This accounts for a certain tendency to diffuseness.[65]

If you have followed the advice given at the beginning of never starting to type until you have got clear in your mind the legal basis of your client's claim, you should know what has to be established in law for the action to succeed and, hence, what has to be stated in the condescendence before the action can be regarded as relevant. Of perhaps greater importance, you will also know what is not essential and can therefore be left out. All you then have to do is type out the essential facts and grounds of action in a logical order, avoiding all frills.

The condescendence is divided into numbered paragraphs, normally called 'articles of condescendence'. The following roadmap may be useful:

- Article one should deal with the parties and jurisdiction.
- Article two should deal with the facts.
- Article three should deal with the legal basis/bases for the action, divided, if necessary, into the common law and statutory case.
- Article four should deal with loss.

---

[65] R W Millar, "Civil Pleading in Scotland", *Michigan Law Review*, vol. 30, no. 4, 1932, 545–581 at 561–562.

- And article five should explain why the action is necessary.[66]

That is the goal. It will not always work out that way, and in some cases it would be positively detrimental to the pleadings to stick rigidly to it. If there are multiple defenders, for example, it is usually appropriate to describe the basis of the action as against each of them in separate articles of condescendence. If there is a case grounded on common law liability and another on breach of statutory duty, it may assist to separate out those different grounds of fault. And of course, you will occasionally have a case where the relevant facts are simply so voluminous, and the grounds of fault so complicated, that there are justifiably many more articles of condescendence than just five or six, or an article of condescendence broken down into lettered or numbered sub-paragraphs. But those cases should genuinely be few and far between.

Start off by identifying the parties. Avoid saying 'Parties are as designed in the instance'. The instance is primarily for the benefit of the postman. Article one of condescendence, on the other hand, is where you introduce the parties. You should explain who the pursuer is and who the defender is, where they reside or where the defender company is based and give such other preliminary information as might be necessary (e.g. that the defender was, at the material time, the pursuer's employer). Mention the ground of jurisdiction, including any special ground such as arrestment or ownership of heritable property.

Then in the second (and possibly subsequent) articles of condescendence, you outline in chronological order the facts

---

[66] This roadmap applies principally to 'standard' (i.e. not commercial or personal injuries) actions. You should have regard to the appropriate court rules and forms for special causes. For example, the form of writ or summons in a personal injuries action stipulates what is to be averred in each statement of claim (as articles of condescendence are known). See Chapter 5.

out of which your client's claim arises. The royal advice to the White Rabbit is still worth following: "'Where shall I begin, please, your Majesty?" asked the White Rabbit. "Begin at the beginning," the King said gravely, "and go on till you come to the end: then stop."'[67]

Suppose the action is one for implement of a contract or damages for breach of contract. You obviously begin by describing the contract. If it is an oral contract, you should give details of when and where it was concluded, and what the parties agreed. If it is in writing, simply give the date of the document (or documents) in which it is embodied and a very brief description of the nature of the contract, e.g. 'By emails dated 16 February 2024 and 4 May 2024, the pursuer contracted to buy and the defender to sell for the price of £6,000 a gold-plated hamster cage'. Having thus identified the documents and given a brief indication of their contents, be sure to go on to incorporate their full terms into the pleadings as follows: 'The terms of the said letters are incorporated and repeated herein' (normally, but unnecessarily, followed by *brevitatis causa* [or 'for the sake of brevity']. Incorporation, in appropriate circumstances, is important. Many contract disputes boil down to straightforward questions of the interpretation of the contract and accordingly can be disposed of at a debate without enquiry into the facts. However, if you have merely quoted bits of the contract and have not incorporated its terms into the pleadings, the sheriff or judge technically cannot look at the contract even if it has been lodged in process, unless a joint minute has been agreed dispensing with the proof of the documents.[68] But beware of the wholesale incorporation into

[67] L Carroll, *Alice's Adventures in Wonderland* (1933).
[68] See *Eadie Cairns v Programmed Maintenance Painting* 1987 SLT 777. This may seem to be a particularly fussy rule and the applicability of some of the *dicta* in *Eadie Cairns* to the modern world of pleading has been questioned (e.g. *Grier v Lord Advocate* [2021] CSOH 18, 2021 SLT 371 at para 39 per Lord Tyre).

the pleadings of a lengthy document, only parts of which are relevant; and be especially wary of incorporating reports from skilled witnesses expressing an opinion.[69] If your case is that there were design or construction defects in a building erected for your client by the defender, you will probably have (and you certainly should have) an independent architect's report detailing the various defects. The basis of your claim, however, is not the architect's report but simply the defender's breach of the express or implied terms of his contract with your client.

Of course, if you are not actually founding on a document as the basis or one of the bases of your case, there is no need to incorporate its terms into the pleadings or even to refer to it at all. But any document you do refer to in the pleadings should be lodged in process at the same time.[70]

Once you have described the oral or written contract in general terms, you should in the same article explain what went wrong. Again, keep this short and simple, using straightforward language. If 'the door of the gold-plated hamster cage was incapable of being securely fastened', just say that. Don't say: 'After a long day, the pursuer had a cup of tea while listening to the Rest Is Politics podcast[71] only to discover that Rupert the hamster was running across the living room floor having escaped from his cage owing to a fault in the design of the door'. The former might be met with an admission; the latter most certainly would not.

Once all relevant facts have been averred, in your next article of condescendence you should refer expressly to any provision of the contract on which you particularly rely which will

---

[69] Such a practice was described by Lord President Carloway as 'usually ... an indicator of indolence' ("How To Win Your Case: What the Court Expects from Advocates" (n 30)). See also *Royal Bank of Scotland Plc v Holmes* 1999 SLT 563.

[70] Ordinary Cause Rules 1993 ("OCR") ch 21; Rules of the Court of Session 1994 ("RCS") ch 27.

[71] Other podcasts are available.

usually be the term that you claim the defender has breached. If it is not too long, set it out in full, or at least set out *verbatim* the important parts of it. If you are relying not on an express but on an implied term, you should state clearly what you say the implied term was, e.g. 'It was an implied term of the contract that the defenders would design and construct the gold-plated hamster cage in accordance with the care, skill and competency reasonably to be expected from experienced professional hamster cage providers. In particular, it was an implied term that the hamster cage would be designed and constructed in a manner which prevented the hamster from escaping the cage'. If you are founding on a statutory implied term, you should specify the Act and the section, e.g. 'Implied terms about the quality of the gold-plated hamster cage were included in the contract. Section 9 of the Consumer Rights Act 2015 provides that every contract to supply goods is to be treated as including a term that the quality of the goods is satisfactory...', and so on, referencing any other relevant statutory provisions along the way. Having done so, you proceed to set out how the defender breached those contractual terms: you narrate the abject failure of the cage door mechanism to keep the hamster securely within its cage.

The next article should deal with the damage or loss your client has suffered and what it has cost (or is likely to cost) to put it right.

And in the final article of condescendence you simply state that the defender has been called upon to pay up and that, because he refuses or delays to do so, the action is necessary.

Some general points may now be made on the 'relevancy' and 'fair notice' essentials.

The 'relevancy' essential
As you will remember, the question of relevancy is determined by assuming that the pursuer proves everything she sets out to prove, and then asking the question: in these circumstances,

does the law give her the remedy she seeks?[72] If it doesn't, then the action is irrelevant and can be dismissed at debate without any evidence having been led. Taking a pursuer to debate on the question of relevancy amounts in essence to the defender saying: 'So what? Even if the pursuer is right about all of this, she isn't entitled to that particular remedy from me'. So the pursuer who says that he was harassed by the defender on an occasion last July, and who seeks damages as a result of that harassment under section 8 of the Protection from Harassment Act 1997, is bound to face a debate on the relevancy on the basis that the 1997 Act only bites if there was harassment on at least two occasions. The pursuer only offering to prove that he was harassed on one occasion, the action would be bound to fail.

An averment which is essential to a party's case, i.e. one which has got to be made before an action of a particular type will be relevant as matter of law, must be stated in clear and outright terms. It is not enough in an action seeking reparation for damage to property to say 'Believed and averred that the defender shot the pursuer's partridge and chopped down his pear tree'. There are circumstances where a 'believed and averred' is appropriate – mainly in respect of an inference which the pursuer draws from primary facts which he has already stated, or in respect of non-essential facts, which are within the defender's knowledge but outwith the pursuer's.[73] But in respect of essential facts, or any facts within the pursuer's own knowledge, 'believed and averred' is not good enough.[74]

Your condescendence must stand on its own feet. If the relevancy of your case is challenged, you cannot rely upon

---

[72] *JD v Lothian Health Board* (n 9) at para 33 per Lord Brodie. Traditionalists may prefer *Jamieson v Jamieson* [1952] AC 525.

[73] *Magee v Bracewell Harrison & Coton* 1980 SLT (Notes) 102. See also *Burnett v Menzies Dougal WS* [2005] CSIH 67, 2006 SC 93.

[74] *McCrone v MacBeth Currie & Co* 1968 SLT (Notes) 24.

substantive averments or explanations made by the defender in the answers unless you have admitted those averments.[75]

The 'fair notice' essential
So much for the 'relevancy' essential. The 'fair notice', or 'specification' essential requires that in drafting your condescendence you should go beyond merely stating facts sufficient to make your action relevant in law. So, although terseness is a virtue in pleading, do not let it get to extremes. Notice has to be given to the defender of all facts which you intend to establish and all grounds of action upon which you propose to rely. If there has to be a proof, you will not (unless your opponent is asleep) be allowed to lead evidence of facts for which you have no record and you will not be allowed to rely on any ground of fault which you have not pled (unless you are allowed to amend – which is unlikely at that stage of an action and can be very expensive, especially if the proof is discharged as a result).

In a reparation action involving the running down of a pedestrian by a motorist, you can state a case which is relevant in law without mentioning that the driver was as drunk as a skunk or that he was later convicted of 19 road traffic offences. But if you intend to lead evidence that he was drunk and later convicted,[76] you must give notice of this in your pleadings. Similarly, in an action for damages you must specify all of the grounds of fault or all of the breaches of contract that you intend to rely upon. Plead the general duty that was owed followed by the specific duties. Your action would probably be relevant as long as you stated just one breach of duty or one breach of contract. But if you have more than one string to your bow (and in a reparation action you almost invariably will

---

[75] *Lee v National Coal Board* 1955 SC 151.

[76] As you are entitled to do under section 10 of the Law Reform (Miscellaneous Provisions) (Scotland) Act 1968. See *Towers v Flaws* [2015] CSIH 97, 2020 SC 209 for a discussion of the effect of this provision.

have), make sure in the pleadings that the defender knows it. And remember the other reason, fair notice aside, for ensuring that your pleadings are sufficiently specific: pleading an otherwise non-essential, but still relevant, fact may allow you to recover documents under a commission and diligence, and a call in a specification of documents will not be approved unless you have averred facts which lay a foundation for the recovery of the documents in question.

However, it is important to stress that it is only the facts and grounds of action that you must or should pled. As has already been discussed, you need not, and you should not, refer in the pleadings to the evidence by which you are going to establish those facts. So in a road traffic, property-damage action, you only need to plead that 'the defender lost control of his car and crashed it into the pursuer's award-winning hedge'; you don't add, 'which was witnessed by Robert Black while he was taking his dog for a walk'. The latter is how you will prove the former – by calling Robert Black as a witness – and is therefore evidence of the fact, rather than the fact itself. Equally, while you plead duties and how they were breached, you do not plead law.[77]

Just how much specification is necessary in any particular case will depend on its circumstances, who the other party is, what the other party is aware of and what the other party may be taken to understand.[78] Material facts – e.g. dates, the names of allegedly negligent employees (if known) for whom

---

[77] But note that, as with the earlier hamster-cage example, you do plead statutory provisions. In petitions for judicial review, it is common to plead law and to cite authorities. It is also competent to do this in commercial actions. See Chapter 5. Note also that you *do* plead foreign law because foreign law is treated as a fact to be proved. For a recent discussion of pleading foreign law, see *Benkert UK Ltd v Paint Dispensing Ltd* [2022] CSIH 55, 2023 SLT 19.

[78] *Richards v Pharmacis Ltd* [2018] CSIH 31, 2018 SLT 492 at para 14 per Lord Brodie.

the defender is vicariously liable, previous accidents, insofar as relevant to foreseeability, and details of losses – should be specified. But it need not be taken too far; just ensure that notice is given of the broad chapters of evidence that you will elicit in support of your client's case.[79] More and more, the courts are taking a pragmatic approach to the assessment of what is required by fair notice and are taking a relatively dim view of defenders complaining that they have not received fair notice owing to a lack of specification in the pleadings,[80] in the absence of some identifiable and material prejudice.

Four final points:

1. There may be no objection to a pursuer making alternative and even inconsistent averments of fact, provided the competing versions are clearly shown to be alternative and the circumstances are such that the pursuer cannot be expected to plump for only one version and stick to it (e.g. because the facts are not within his knowledge).[81] In a reparation action, for example, the pursuer may be in no position to say exactly how the accident happened. All you can do then is set out the possible ways in which it could have happened and plead that each one of these possibilities involved fault on the part of the defender. The main danger of pleading facts in the alternative (as opposed to having alternative grounds of fault) is that the overall relevancy of your action is tested by reference to the weakest of your alternatives, since it is only that version that the pursuer absolutely offers to prove. This is known as the 'weaker alternative rule' and it has struck fear into the hearts of generations of lawyers.

---

[79] What is required in abbreviated pleadings is considered in Chapter 5.
[80] See, e.g. *Chalmers v Diageo Scotland Ltd* [2024] CSIH 2.
[81] *Finnie v Logie* (1859) 21 D 825 at 829 per the Lord President (McNeill).

But it is nothing to be afraid of.[82] As Lord Stott – whose explanation of the rule is cited to this day – said,

> The … rule is not a piece of procedural mumbo jumbo; it is based on logic and common sense. If legal liability arises only on proof that the fact is A and if all that a pursuer offers to prove is that it is either A or B his pleadings are irrelevant. The relevancy of the case is tested on the weaker alternative.[83]

More recently, Lord Stewart explained it in this way:

> The weaker alternative rule is capable of being misunderstood … The logic of the rule is this: someone who will not commit to proving the truth of a relevant factual basis for his or her claim cannot insist on what might turn out to be a pointless fact-finding inquiry. The deficiency struck at by the weaker alternative rule lies in the refusal to choose between relevant and irrelevant bases of claim; and it is this that sabotages the claim as a whole.[84]

The rule, therefore, only bites if, on one of the alternative versions, no legal liability would arise, and the case is tested by reference to the case which is the weaker in law. In other words, if a pursuer does not put his eggs in just one factual basket, then he had better be capable of explaining why the defender would be liable regardless of which set of facts is proved. There is no bar, however, to pleading alternative and inconsistent factual cases, if otherwise relevant, unless to do so would be incompatible with substantial justice.[85] Equally, there is of course no harm (and there can be great advantage)

---

[82] And the law reports suggest that most attempts to rely upon it are doomed.

[83] *Haigh & Ringrose Ltd v Barrhead Builders Ltd* 1981 SLT 157 at 157 per Lord Stott.

[84] *Greig v Davidson* [2015] CSOH 44, 2015 SCLR 722 at para 20 per Lord Stewart.

[85] *Ibid* at para 10.

in pleading multiple grounds of action or fault based upon the one set of facts. But in that case, you should consider whether to plead them cumulatively rather than alternatively. Any second and cumulative ground of action should begin with: 'Further, …'. 'Further, and in any event…' denotes an alternative ground. '*Separatim*' can also be used. While it is often said that '*separatim*' is to be deployed only when what follows contradicts what has come before, there is no reason for that to be so. It simply means 'separately' and can therefore be used to introduce alternative, contradictory or indeed complementary facts or grounds of action. So long as it is made clear to the reader which one it is, it shouldn't matter. Given the pitfalls, you should never clutter up your pleadings with alternative versions of the facts unless it is absolutely necessary. If you have no choice, make it clear to the reader that you are about to plead an alternative case by use of the easy-to-remember signifier: 'Alternatively' or '*Separatim*' … , and for clarity, you should plead your alternative case in a separate article of condescendence.

2. '*Esto*' is used to engage with a disputed hypothesis. It might be that you want to respond to something that the defender is likely to say against you, or it may be that you want to engage with the possibility that what you have pled already is incorrect. In either case, you commence that section of your pleading with '*Esto*'. For example: '*Esto* the defender did not intentionally shoot the pursuer's partridge, he failed to take reasonable care when discharging his firearm and is liable to the pursuer for the consequences of his negligence'.

   With the exception of such 'standard' terms, do not litter your pleadings with old-fashioned language. Write simply and write plainly. You will not suffer a technical defeat for a failure to deploy Latin!

3. Whatever you do, do not just copy out into your condescendence the pursuer's precognition (or, worse still, your rough notes of what he said to you when you interviewed him). The first Lord Clyde, while still at the Bar, said once in the course of a lecture: 'Too many condescendences

find their way into type without ever having passed
through the crucible of the pleader's mind'.[86] There may
still be some truth in this. If you are engaged in a court
practice, there will inevitably be some pleaders whose
handiwork you will be able to recognise immediately and
will come to dread encountering, since their condescendences invariably consist of pages and pages of what seem
to be extracts from very lengthy, rambling precognitions
or copied and pasted paragraphs from their own opin-
ions. This is the aforementioned 'Stream of Consciousness
Pleading'. It may be due, in some measure, to pleadings
being dictated or 'bashed out' quickly, which can have
the effect of encouraging the pleader to say the first thing
that comes into their head without considering either the
sense of what they are saying or the order in which (even
if it is nonsense) they ought to be saying it. Except in the
very simplest debt-recovery case, we would advise against
dictating your pleadings unless you have first sketched out
fairly fully what you want to say and are satisfied both
with its content and with its arrangement. And under no
circumstances should you use, that agency of the devil, AI!
Be careful about using 'firm styles' without tailoring them
and giving careful thought to what the case in front of you
requires. At the very least, remember to fill in the blanks
and remove any references to the poor client of the firm
from 35 years ago whose writ became the style!

4.   Do not overstate your case in your pleadings. It goes without saying that you must never aver facts for which you
have no evidence 'in the hope that something may turn
up in the course of a case to justify them'.[87] That would

---

[86] J A Clyde, "Practice and Procedure in the Court of Session" (1907)
18 Jur Rev 319 at 326.

[87] *Boustead v Gardner* (1879) 7 R 139 at 145 per the Lord Justice Clerk
(Moncfrieff). See also *JD v Lothian Health Board* (n 9) at para 30 per
Lord Brodie.

be highly improper. And you should certainly always be very careful indeed about making averments of fraud or bad faith.[88] You are not just a mouth-piece for your client. Indeed, in drafting pleadings, a solicitor or advocate takes on 'an office in the performance of which he owes a duty, not to his client only, but also to the court, to the members of his own profession, and to the public'.[89] You have been warned!

While the above advice is aimed principally at 'standard' actions – i.e. not the special causes, the specific requirements of which are dealt with in Chapter 5 – what is said is of general applicability and can be adapted to any form of pleading. It may of course be more difficult to decide what has to go into the condescendence in more exotic types of action, but if you have got clear in your mind what your ground of action is and what the law on the subject is, the problem of what facts you must incorporate in order to plead a relevant case should be fairly easily resolved. As before, you can often get assistance or confirmation of the views which you have formed by consulting a book of styles which may contain a specimen condescendence for the type of action you want to raise.

(f) The pleas-in-law

These take the form of short legal propositions specifically applicable to the facts of the case. They are statements of the legal grounds upon which the pursuer, in the circumstances stated in the condescendence, is entitled to the remedy or remedies set forth in the crave:

> The stating of appropriate pleas-in-law remains a cornerstone of the system of written pleadings, designed primarily ... to give any defender fair notice of the legal case against him

[88] On all of which, see Chapter 6.
[89] *Batchelor v Pattison and Mackersy* (1876) 3 R 914 at 918 per the Lord President (Inglis).

and to state to the court the legal basis upon which the action proceeds.[90]

So, from a glance at the pleas-in-law, it should be clear whether the action is based on delict or contract or the Human Rights Act, and by reading the craves followed immediately by the pleas-in-law, the reader should be in no doubt at all as to what the pursuer wants and why she is entitled to it. As already noted and as will be discussed in Chapter 5, there are now some types of procedure which have abandoned pleas-in-law, notably personal injuries actions and the simple procedure.[91] But that does not mean that you can pass over this section if you practise exclusively in the field of personal injury. While the pleas-in-law themselves may have gone from the writ in such actions, the propositions of law upon which they are based are frequently now to be found in the final article of condescendence. More importantly, the basic principles of pleading have not changed, and all actions require both to be relevant and to provide fair notice, and it is entirely possible that a personal injuries action will go to debate on matters such as relevancy and specification, competence, jurisdiction, time-bar and so on.

There should be at least one plea-in-law addressed to every substantive part of the crave. You should be able to direct the court to the particular averments which support a particular plea-in-law. If there are no such averments, the plea-in-law is liable to be repelled. A plea that asks for decree to be granted as craved because the defender 'acted as condescended upon'

---

[90] *Kelly Ltd v Capital Bank plc* 2004 SLT 483 at para 13 per Lord Carloway.

[91] It may also be permissible to jettison pleas-in-law in certain commercial actions, e.g. those dealing solely with the construction of a document. See: OCR ch 40; RCS ch 47; and Court of Session Practice Note No 1 of 2017. Petitions in the Court of Session contain a 'prayer' rather than pleas-in-law, except petitions for judicial review.

is 'so vague as to be meaningless'.[92] If you are founding on alternative grounds of action, these must be distinguished by separate pleas-in-law, with all but the first being prefaced with '*Separatim...*'. When a plea is needed to deal with an argument made against you or which proceeds on the hypothesis that your primary position is incorrect, it is prefaced with '*Esto...*' (e.g., '*Esto* the action is time-barred, it should be permitted to proceed in terms of section 19A of the Prescription and Limitation (Scotland) Act 1973'). A plea prefaced with '*Separatim, esto...*' should probably be avoided on the basis that it can almost always be dealt with by use of either '*Separatim*' **or** '*Esto*'. You do not, however, need pleas-in-law relating to expenses or to any warrants which you are seeking (such as to arrest on the dependence or to intimate to 'connected persons'). It is best practice to insert a plea covering any *interim* order that you want (e.g. *interim* interdict).

Follow *Macphail*'s advice[93] on the order of the pursuer's pleas-in-law: first, the pleas which are claimed to justify a decision in the pursuer's favour; then the pleas which refute the defender's substantive case; and finally, the pleas dealing with the relevancy of the defences. Of course, it will not be possible to insert any pleas dealing with the defender's case until the defences have been lodged, something which may never be necessary (or possible) if the action is undefended. We touch on those pleas in Chapter 3.

In respect of most of the everyday types of action such as debt recovery, damages for breach of contract, delivery of corporeal moveables and family actions, the form of the appropriate pleas-in-law for the pursuer has been hallowed by tradition. So too has the order of pleas. All you have to do is look up *Green's Litigation Styles*. Indeed, most of the pleas you are ever likely to need, even in fairly unusual classes of action, are to be found in *Green's*. But

---

[92] *CSG Commercial Ltd v AJ Capital Partners LLC* [2022] CSOH 60, 2022 SLT 1345 at para 22 per Lord Braid.
[93] *Sheriff Court Practice*, ch 9, para 9.112.

if there does not appear to be one which exactly fits the bill in your client's case, make one up yourself, but be cautious in so doing. It is, however, not too difficult so long as you are familiar with the standard form pleas and if you remember that what you are doing is formulating a proposition of law which, applied to the parties to your case, entitles the pursuer to decree in terms of the crave or of some part of the crave.

So that's the writ.

All that remains to be said is this. Draft your pleadings to assist, rather than to irritate, the court. That applies both to choice of language and to presentation. Certain phrases are bound to irritate; 'further explained and averred', 'as hereinafter…' or 'as hereinbefore condescended upon' were the particular bugbears of Lord President Carloway.[94] To that list, we would add 'the pursuer alighted the vehicle'[95] and 'the defender's averments in answer are specifically denied'. Be extremely cautious before littering your pleadings with defined terms. If the only statute averred in the writ is the Occupiers' Liability (Scotland) Act 1960, there is absolutely no need to add in parenthesis 'hereinafter, "the 1960 Act"'; nor is there a need to say 'The pursuer is Robert Black ("the pursuer")'. If for whatever reason you feel that you have no choice but to use defined terms (which could only really be because the pleadings would be otherwise incomprehensible) use them sparingly and make sure that they are deployed consistently – including as between the parties.[96] Finally, endeavour to make the writ easy to read.

---

[94] "How to Win Your Case: What the Court Expects from Advocates" (n 30).

[95] The favoured phrase of police officer witnesses and pleaders alike. Why not: 'the pursuer got out of his car'?

[96] Which you can do during the adjustment period: see Chapter 4. In *Parks of Hamilton (Townhead Garage) Ltd v Deas* [2022] SAC (Civ) 18, 2022 SCLR 292, a consumer action, one party referred to the vehicle at the centre of the dispute as 'the car' while the other referred to it as 'the Used MIG Vehicle'.

It may be best not to deviate from Arial, Times New Roman or – the Scottish legal profession's favourite – Palatino Linotype. Stick to font size 12. Use at least 1.5 line spacing. And while the use of headings is unnecessary most of the time, if an action is particularly complicated factually and the subject of various "chapters" in separate articles of condescendence, headings may actually help rather than hinder.[97]

If you follow the advice in this chapter, you may get through your career without receiving a judgment with a paragraph such as this:

> In this action, the record consists of 62 pages of averments, many of which are typed in small font size with minimal line spacing. There has been little attempt over these 62 pages to present the pleadings in any recognisable order; much evidence is pled, there is no consistent chronological sequence to the averments and no discernible attempt to lay out the averments in a manner which might focus the issues upon which the court is asked to adjudicate. Identifying with precision what is agreed and where parties differ has been an almost impossible task. Identifying what is material and what is peripheral in the long and cumbersome narratives is yet more challenging. Many averments consist of lengthy sentences containing numerous statements of fact. Article 16 of Condescendence extends to 37 separate paragraphs over 8 pages. The approach to Article 16 is mirrored in many of the 22 Articles.[98]

Ouch!

---

[97] We appreciate that this is a matter of great controversy.

[98] *Donnelly v South Lanarkshire Council* [2021] SAC (Civ) 30 at para 28 per Sheriff Principal Anwar. In fact, it was the publication of this particular decision which prompted Professor Black to suggest that it was high time for a second edition of this book!

CHAPTER THREE

Drafting the Defences

The document lodged by the party who has been served with the writ is known as the 'defences'. At least that is what it is called when it is an initial writ or a summons which has been served; the document responding to a petition is known as the 'answers' and it is a 'response form' you lodge if served with a simple procedure claim form. But as with the previous chapter, this chapter is concerned primarily with drafting defences to a writ or a summons, while the peculiarities of responding to the other most commonly encountered causes are dealt with in Chapter 4. Of course, many of the suggestions made in the paragraphs which follow apply with the same force regardless of the type of case or the court in which it is raised.

The good news is that the pleadings for the defender are usually easier to draft than those for the pursuer. It is, after all, usually more challenging and onerous to pursue a case than it is to defend one,[1] seeing as it is the pursuer who, by and large, has the burden of proof and who has the particularly daunting task of framing a relevant and sufficiently specific case.

If they are properly framed, the defences will also, at least normally, be considerably shorter, which is always a good start. If the defence is (as it often is, at any event to begin with) that the pursuer has got both the facts and the applicable law hopelessly wrong, then it does not take many words to say so.

Even if the defender has preliminary pleas (e.g., all parties not called, incompetency, irrelevancy) he is bound also to

---

[1] Even if the consequences of the defender losing may be graver than those the pursuer will face if she loses.

disclose his defence on the merits of the case (e.g., that he does not owe the debt; that he was not negligent). It is incompetent to seek to withhold disclosure of one's position on the merits of the pursuer's claim until such time as a preliminary plea has been disposed of,[2] with the sole and important exception of a plea of no jurisdiction; in that case and in that case only, the rules of court permit a defender who wishes to contest the jurisdiction of the court to lodge defences which deal solely with that question and which do not respond to the substantive averments.[3]

The main problem in drafting defences is not any difficulty in mastering the proper technique in doing so, but rather the less than ideal conditions under which you may find yourself having to operate. There can be no bricks without straw, but a distressingly high proportion of defenders expect their legal advisers to be able to draft knock-out defences without facts or information, including as to what their defence to the pursuer's perfectly crafted action actually is.

The defences

Defences start with the heading 'DEFENCES in the action at the instance of[4] AB (designed), **Pursuer** against XY (designed) **Defender**'. If you are but one of a number of defenders, make it clear to which party the defences belong (e.g., 'DEFENCES for the TENTH DEFENDER…'). The operative part of the defences then follows and is divided into two sections:

(a)   Answers to the pursuer's condescendence
(b)   Pleas-in-law for the defender

---

[2] *Thorburn v Dempster* (1900) 2 F 583.
[3] OCR r 9.1(1)(a) and (2); RCS r 18.2(1)(b). Indeed, if contesting jurisdiction the defences must not deal with the substance.
[4] Or '*in causa*'.

In family actions, where the defender is seeking certain orders, the defences will in addition contain a crave (or craves) or conclusion (or conclusions) for the defender.[5]

The answers

Here you have to respond to the pursuer's averments. You do it in numbered paragraphs corresponding to the numbered articles of the condescendence (or statement of claim or statement of facts).[6] Take each article of condescendence in turn. Pick out the averments which the defender has told you he accepts, and admit them by repeating the averment prefixed by the phrase 'Admitted that…'. Any of the pursuer's averments of fact which are outwith the defender's knowledge should be said to be 'not known and not admitted'. If a fact is outwith the defender's knowledge but he nevertheless believes it to be true (and it is not a fact which harms his case in any way) you can say 'Believed to be true that …'. But you must be certain before you use 'believed to be true' instead of 'not known and not admitted' that the fact in question is not crucial to the pursuer's case, since 'believed to be true' is equivalent to an admission and dispenses with the necessity of the pursuer proving the averment in question.[7]

Having dealt with admissions and with 'not known and not admitted's, you are left with the remainder of the pursuer's averments which, according to the defender, are not true. You respond to them in a comprehensive and summary fashion by resorting to the time-honoured formula '*Quoad ultra* denied', which just means that everything else, i.e. every other averment of the pursuer not expressly dealt with by an admission or a not known or not admitted, is denied. There is no need to add 'except insofar as coinciding herewith', albeit it can, on occasion, be a useful add-on where a pursuer is responding

---

[5] See OCR ch 33; and RCS ch 49. A general introduction to pleadings in family cases is found in Chapter 5.

[6] Answers to a petition in the Court of Session *do* have pleas-in-law; the prayer is not directly responded to.

[7] *Scottish NE Railway v Napier* (1859) 21 D 700.

to explanations made by a defender[8] – something covered in the chapter on adjustments – or where a defender risks inadvertently admitting some aspect of the pursuer's narrative.[9] It is also sometimes seen where the pursuer has pled a lengthy narrative and the defender wishes to plead his own narrative, some but nothing like all of which will coincide with the pursuer's; in that case, the 'except insofar as coinciding herewith' is deployed almost as an explanation for the fact that there ought to have been some admissions. This practice is best avoided. It makes it harder for the court to know precisely what is disputed and what is not and it is contrary to the requirement to admit what you must admit. On a presentational matter, make sure that '*quoad ultra*' is italicised or at least underlined; not only is it customary to italicise Latin, but more importantly it will greatly assist you (and, more importantly, the judge) later on in identifying, at a glance, where the defender's pleadings move on from dealing with the pursuer's case to dealing with its own case.

That, in brief outline, is how it should always be done: first of all, admit specifically all averments in the particular article of condescendence which your client has told you are true; next comes 'believed to be true' in those relatively rare cases where it can be safely and appropriately used; then use the 'not known and not admitted' formula specifically in respect of each averment which is outwith the defender's knowledge; and end up with a general, blanket denial of everything else. Do not just take every sentence of the condescendence as it comes and repeat it with the prefix 'Admitted that', 'Not known and not admitted that' or 'Denied that'. That inevitably has the result of making the pleadings a sloppy guddle in which you flounder here, there and everywhere trying vainly to find out what facts the parties are at issue on. Do all your admissions first, then all your 'not known and not admitteds' and conclude with a general denial of the rest. Even if it seems the easiest approach at the time, you should never reverse the procedure and have

---

[8] *Campbell v Campbell* (1863) 1 M 217.
[9] *Music Hire Service (Manchester) Ltd v Roccio* 1961 SLT (Notes) 13.

specific denials followed by a general admission – '*quoad ultra* admitted'. If you do, you can be sure that at adjustment the pursuer will quietly insert a couple of nasty little averments which you would not dream of admitting and which would, if you had followed the correct procedure, have been covered by your general denial. That is a risk which is never worth taking. Of course, if everything the pursuer says is true, the only response you need to make is the one word 'Admitted'. This often happens in respect of the first article of condescendence which simply identifies the parties, and sometimes also in respect of the narrative of the conclusion of a contract or the happening of an accident. If there is nothing to deny, but there are averments which are outwith the defender's knowledge, you should conclude with '*Quoad ultra* not known and not admitted'. The one word 'Denied' is appropriate where all of the averments are of facts which are within the defender's knowledge and which are said by him to be untrue or are of grounds of fault which the defender denies. But as we shall see later on in our discussion of skeleton (or skeletal) defences, bare denials can be dangerous if the defender does not go on to provide some explanation or a competing version of the facts.

Sometimes you will see a defender specifically deny a particular averment made by the pursuer. It is most frequently seen in response to what is seen as *the* crucial averment or because the averment is such a wounding or outrageous one (e.g. 'It is specifically denied that the defender trained Rupert the hamster to escape from the cage and return to the defender so that he could be sold again'). Do not do this. And resist any entreaties from your client to do this. So long as there is a general denial it is completely unnecessary, and it makes you a mere mouth-piece for your client. One of the advantages of lawyers representing litigants is to take the heat out of a fractious and emotionally wrought dispute. Leave the specific denials to party litigants.

You may also encounter (though, again, you should never use yourself) the expression 'Denied as stated'. This seems to be intended to convey that what the pursuer has averred is not wholly fictional, but that his averments contain some distortions or inaccuracies or some unjustified inferences which he is seeking to draw from the facts as stated by him. In such circumstances, instead of saying 'denied as stated' you should simply admit the facts which the pursuer has accurately stated (if necessary with an accompanying explanation or qualification) and deal with the rest by way of your general denial. For example, if the pursuer avers that 'this court has jurisdiction because it was within this sheriff court district that the defender kidnapped the pursuer', it is perfectly acceptable to respond: 'Admitted that this court has jurisdiction. *Quoad ultra* denied'. It is equally acceptable to admit certain averments 'under explanation to follow'. This is particularly useful where the defender admits a particular fact which might seem hard to recover from, were matters to be left there. For example, the pursuer may aver 'The defender did not carry out a risk assessment on the day of the accident'. If that is true, but you are told that an assessment of the very activity in question was carried in the days before the accident, then that averment can be admitted 'under explanation to follow'.

It is incumbent upon the defender to answer any statement of fact made by the purser. An unanswered statement of fact (i.e. one that is not expressly admitted or one that is not caught by a general denial) is deemed to be admitted.[10] Any fact averred by the pursuer which is within the defender's knowledge and which is not denied by the defender is held to have been admitted.[11] In relation to such facts, i.e. facts within the defender's knowledge, the response 'No admission is made' is in law equivalent to, and is treated as, an admission.[12] If the pursuer has referred to documents in his condescendence, it is usual for the defender if he cannot, or is not prepared to, admit the existence and the contents of the documents simply to refer to the documents for their terms, 'beyond which no admission is made'.[13] Provided the document is not one which

---

[10] *Scottish NE Railway v Napier* (1859) 21 D 700.
[11] *Pegler v Northern Agricultural Implement Co* (1877) 4 R 435; OCR r 9.7.
[12] *Clark v Clark* 1967 SLT 108.
[13] *Pringle v Bremner and Stirling* (1867) 5 M (HL) 55.

the defender can be expected to have personal knowledge of (e.g. it was not written by him or sent to him), such a reference does not amount even to an admission that the document exists or ever existed. It is an expression normally used, however, when the pursuer references a document and immediately advances a construction of the document with which the defender is either uncomfortable or positively rejects. What the defender reads the document to mean can be explained later on in the pleadings. If you are genuinely questioning the very existence of the document which the pursuer has referred to, it is good practice (though not strictly essential) to refer for its terms to 'the alleged document' and not to 'the said document'. But rather than leaving matters there, you should go on to explain what your client's position actually is in respect of the document in question.[14] The expression '…is referred to for its terms beyond which no admission is made' is also often used by defenders when responding to a statutory case of fault, e.g. 'the Diving at Work Regulations 1997 are referred to for their terms beyond which no admission is made'.[15]

After you have answered all of the averments in a particular article of condescendence, you should go on at the end to provide any explanation or qualifications or to state any additional facts which are necessary to support the defender's case. You preface these with the expression 'Explained and averred that…'. Generally speaking you should only be offering an explanation to the averments made by the pursuer in the corresponding article of condescendence which you are answering. The one exception to this is if you are responding to a

---

[14] Macphail, *Sheriff Court Practice*, ch 9, para 9.75.

[15] See *English v North Lanarkshire Council* 1999 SCLR 310 for a discussion as to whether that is an implied admission of the applicability of the statutory provision. Lord Reed held that where the applicability of a statutory provision depends on a particular state of facts, the defenders' failure to give notice that those facts are in dispute may have the consequence that they are not allowed to raise the issue (at p 326). His Lordship went on, however, to 'deprecate any tendency towards artificiality and technicality in such matters'.

poorly drafted writ in which the facts and grounds of fault are split between many tens of unnecessary articles of condescendence. In that case, it is acceptable (and indeed preferable) for the defender to provide its response to each chapter of the pursuer's case in just one of the answers, and as necessary to refer back to that answer later in the defences. If an explanation or qualification relates specifically to a particular averment made by the pursuer, then, provided the explanation is a short one, it is often convenient to tack it on to the response to the averment in question and not to place it on its own at the end of the answer (e.g. 'Admitted that the canary sold and delivered by the defender to the pursuer did not sing, under explanation that the canary, as the pursuer well knew, was stuffed').

You will need to incorporate explanations into your answers if you have a substantive defence, e.g. that the accident was caused or materially contributed to by the pursuer's own fault, or that the pursuer is not entitled to payment because she did not finish (or did not do properly) the work which she was employed to do. You should add explanations to your answers to the pursuer's averments only if it is necessary to do so in order *either* to provide the foundation for a substantive defence *or* to give the pursuer fair notice of the line of defence which will be taken, and of facts which the defender will seek to establish at proof. The same obligation of fair notice rests on the defender as on the pursuer.[16] But do not go around putting in explanations if you do not have to. Do not volunteer information for the sake of it. If your defence is simply that the pursuer has got her facts wrong, content yourself with denying her version and saying so. Be wary of being drawn into arguments with the pursuer or rebutting every allegation, however eccentric, that is thrown at you. Do not be lured into explaining why the pursuer's version simply cannot be correct. Just as in cross-examination, so in drafting defences: there is an art in knowing where and when to stop.

In all of this, bear in mind that the court will not, in general, sustain a ground of defence which is not stated on record, and

---

[16] *McNaught v British Railways Board* 1979 SLT (News) 99.

the court will not permit evidence to be led to rebut the pursuer's case in the absence of pleadings. Any statutory defence must be pled. And remember the situations where the burden of proof falls on the defender, such as in advancing a plea of contributory negligence, the defence of truth in defamation proceedings[17] or where a statutory obligation is subject to an exception (e.g. to do something as far as is 'reasonably practicable').[18]

Finally, a word on skeleton defences. These consist of bare denials of every averment made by the pursuer, sometimes even going so far as to deny the identification of the parties in article one of condescendence. Skeleton defences are very common. Often they are the only kind that can be lodged, given the time-limits within which defences have to be prepared. It frequently takes a considerable time for a defender to gather together the information which will be necessary to make a full and detailed reply to the pursuer's averments. And you must never admit any averment, no matter how apparently innocuous, until your client has confirmed to you that the averment is accurate. In such circumstances, if the defences are to be lodged in time at all, skeleton defences can often be the only solution. This is usually fine,[19] so long as the client is informed that the information necessary to put flesh on the bones will have to be obtained and supplied by him as soon as possible and certainly in time to enable the defender's pleadings to be put into a satisfactory state during the adjustment

[17] Defamation and Malicious Publications (Scotland) Act 2021, s 5.
[18] *Nimmo v Alexander Cowan & Sons Ltd* 1967 SC (HL) 79.
[19] Note the terms of Court of Session Practice Note No 1 of 2013 on personal injuries: 'Practitioners are reminded that, unless there is good reason for their deployment, such as incomplete instructions or lack of access to factual information, blanket denials or skeletal defences are not an acceptable starting point in the pleadings. The duty of candour exists at all times and does so to serve both the court and the parties. The court will, ordinarily, bear this in mind when faced with a motion for summary decree'. This should probably be read across to all types of action.

period. That is indeed a preferable course of action to relying upon judicial discretion being exercised in your favour to have the defences received late. If the defences are not bulked up during the adjustment period, and remain uncandid in their responses to positive averments of the pursuer, the defences are irrelevant and the defender is not entitled to put the pursuer to the proof. In such circumstances, the only serious question for the court is whether to grant summary decree.[20]

But if, in reality, the defender has no defence, and knows that he has no defence, and wishes to put in skeleton defences merely as a tactic to delay decree being pronounced against him, this is an abuse of the process of the court and you as a solicitor and an officer owing duties to the court and to the administration of justice should not become a party to it.[21] If skeleton defences have already been lodged by the point in time at which you make this grim discovery, you must withdraw the defences or withdraw from acting.

Pleas-in-law

Whereas in most cases the pursuer will have and will need only one or two pleas, the defender even in relatively straightforward actions will often have five or six. There will almost always be a couple of pleas on the merits (e.g., 'The pursuer's averments so far as material being unfounded in fact, the defender should be assoilzied' or 'The pursuer not having suffered loss and damage as a result of any breach of contractual or other duty of the defender, decree of absolvitor should be pronounced'). There will also often be pleas directed to substantive defences such as the pursuer's sole fault (e.g., 'The escape of water having been caused by the sole fault of the pursuer, decree of absolvitor should be pronounced') or contributory negligence (e.g., '*Esto* the accident was to any extent caused by fault on the part of

---

[20] *Urquhart v Sweeney* 2006 SC 591 at para 41 per the Lord Justice Clerk (Gill). On summary decree in general, see RCS, r 21; OCR r 17; *Henderson v 3052775 Nova Scotia Ltd* 2006 SC (HL) 85.

[21] *Stewart v Stewart* 1984 SLT (Sh Ct) 58; *Russell v Russell* [2017] CSOH 137, 2018 SC 130.

the defender (which is denied), it also having been caused or contributed to by fault on the part of the pursuer, any award of damages should be reduced in terms of s 1 of the Law Reform (Contributory Negligence) Act 1945')[22] or, if there is more than one defender, apportionment (e.g., '*Esto* any loss or damage to the pursuers was caused to any extent through the fault of the first defender (which is denied), it also having been contributed to by the fault of the second defender, the damages, if any, awarded to the pursuer should be apportioned between the first and second defenders in terms of the Law Reform (Miscellaneous Provisions) (Scotland) Act 1940, section 3'). In actions for payment, there will often be a plea that the sum sued for is excessive. You may very well wish to take a plea that the obligation on which the pursuer is suing has been extinguished by prescription.

So you will appreciate how the number of a defender's pleas can mount up. And we have not yet mentioned the whole broad category of preliminary pleas: irrelevancy, lack of specification, incompetency, no jurisdiction, no title to sue, *lis alibi pendens, forum non conveniens*, to name but a few. According to the first Lord President Clyde,

> Those pleas are preliminary which, unless met, lead to the disposal of the action without inquiry into the merits of the dispute which the action is intended to raise. This explains why the plea to relevancy is classed as preliminary: the pleader says: 'What the opposite party says may be true, or it may not, but even if it be assumed that it is all true, nevertheless he cannot prevail against me, either because an essential fact is unrepresented in his averments, or because the facts he avers would not, even if proved, justify the application of the legal principle to which he appeals.' The plea to the relevancy, in short,

---

[22] This is, of course, less commonly encountered nowadays, since most personal injuries do not require pleas-in-law. But it is worth reminding yourself of the common personal injury pleas, since 'complex' personal injuries actions in both the sheriff court and the Court of Session (managed under separate rules of court) *do* require pleas-in-law. See OCR ch 36A, and RCS ch 42A.

avoids, or at least postpones, any joinder of issue on the merits of the case.[23]

If you think that the court has no jurisdiction over the defender, you must take a plea of 'no jurisdiction' at the earliest possible opportunity. If you lodge defences without such a plea, this amounts to a tacit prorogation of the jurisdiction of the court,[24] and any attempt thereafter to add a plea of 'no jurisdiction' by adjustment or amendment comes too late.[25]

In almost every action or petition, a plea to the relevancy will be taken along with a complaint about lack of specification. It is very rare indeed to a find a record which does not contain a plea to the relevancy. Nine times out of ten the plea is never debated and the case goes to proof before answer. The plea is shoved in – we hesitate to say unthinkingly – merely as a matter of form or in the hope against hope that some clever argument will eventually dawn upon the pleader which will allow for a debate at which the action will be dismissed.

In a debate on relevancy, it is worth bearing in mind that it is always for the defender to show that the pursuer must necessarily fail in her action even if all her averments are proved. There is no onus on the pursuer to establish that if she proves all her averments, she is in law bound to succeed.[26] It is also only in the very rarest of cases that a negligence action could properly be dismissed on relevancy without proof being led.[27]

---

[23] R W Millar, "Civil Pleading in Scotland", n 59 at 568.

[24] Erskine, *Institute*, I, ii, 27; *Ward & Co v Samyang Navigation Co* 1975 SC (HL) 26; *Clarke v Fennoscandia Ltd (No 2)* 2001 SLT 1311 at para 27 per Lord Johnston.

[25] Cf. *Fraser-Johnston Engineering Co v Jeffs* 1920 SC 222. This case can be distinguished on its facts; if it cannot, it is simply inconsistent with the authorities (Macphail, *Sheriff Court Practice*, ch 9, fn 403).

[26] *Jamieson v Jamieson*, [1952] AC 525, at 50 per Lord Normand.

[27] *Miller v South of Scotland Electricity Board* 1958 SC (HL) 20. But be warned: cases of dismissal of reparation actions may be very rare, but they are not non-existent: see, for example, *MacDonald v Aberdeenshire Council* [2013] CSIH 83, 2014 SC 114; *David v Powerteam Electrical Services (UK) Ltd* [2023] CSOH 94, 2024 SLT 85.

If you take a plea to the competency, you should disclose the ground of incompetency which you found upon. You may (and perhaps ought to) do that in the plea itself (e.g., 'In respect that the pursuers have combined to claim damages for breach of separate and unrelated contracts with the defender, the action is incompetent and should be dismissed'),[28] or you may take a general plea to the competency ('The action, being incompetent, should be dismissed') and provide specification as to why you say it is incompetent in the body of the defences.

As far as pleas to the relevancy are concerned, a general plea is enough. You do not need to disclose the ground or grounds upon which you claim that the action is irrelevant in the plea itself, but of course any fundamental attack to the legal relevancy of the pursuer's case ought properly to be pled in answers to the condescendence. On a general plea to the relevancy you can argue any relevancy point from the most trivial and easily remedied to the most serious and irremediable.[29] While a plea to the relevancy expressed in such general terms is by far the most commonly encountered, it is perfectly competent (and sometimes proper) to draft a plea which attacks specific averments (e.g., 'The pursuer's averments in article 4 of condescendence relating to the liability of King Charles III being irrelevant, should not be remitted to probation').[30] Bear in mind, however, that if you limit your attack to specific averments, the action as a whole will not be dismissed at debate but the court may excise those specific averments, with the defender thus spared going to proof and having to advance argument on that particular part of the pursuer's case.

A plea directed to lack of specification amounts to a complaint that the pursuer has not given fair notice of the case which the defender has to meet. In modern practice it is normally incorporated into the plea to the relevancy: 'The pursuer's averments being irrelevant *et separatim* lacking in

---

[28] *Coxall v Stewart* 1976 SLT 275.

[29] For an example of the latter, see *X v Brown* [2024] CSIH 6, 2024 SLT 454.

[30] See, e.g., *Bark v Scott* 1954 SC 72.

specification, the action should be dismissed'. If the pursuer's (or the defender's) pleadings are seriously lacking in specification, the action as a whole, or the particular part of the action (or defences), will be irrelevant. As before, it is competent to attack particular articles of condescendence or particular chapters of the pursuer's case as either lacking in specification or being irrelevant and lacking in specification. You could, for example, plead: 'The pursuer's averments in article 5 of condescendence as regards future loss are [irrelevant *et separatim*] lacking in specification and should not be remitted to probation'. But of course, defenders should not take a specification point when the information they complain has not been averred is information within their knowledge but not within the pursuer's knowledge.[31] As already mentioned, the courts are unlikely to be impressed by a defender taking this plea cynically. After all,

> a record should not be subjected to the careful and meticulous scrutiny devoted to a conveyancing deed. The matter must be looked at broadly with a view to ascertaining whether the defenders have been given fair notice of the case which the pursuer intends to prove.[32]

You are more likely to succeed in having an action dismissed as irrelevant on the ground of lack of specification, or in having averments which are excessively general excluded from probation, if in your answers you have made a 'call' upon the pursuer to provide the information in question.[33] A call may be placed in any answer (or in any article of condescendence) and it looks like this: 'The pursuer is called upon to specify the

---

[31] *Macdonald v Glasgow Western Hospitals* 1954 SLT 225 at 231; *Richards v Pharmacia Ltd, c/o Pfizer Ltd* 2018 SLT 492 at paras 47 *et seq* per the Lord Justice Clerk (Dorrian).

[32] *McMenemy v James Dougal & Sons Ltd* 1960 SLT (Notes) 84 at 85 per Lord Guest.

[33] *Bryce v Allied Ironfounders* 1969 SLT (Notes) 29; *M Publications (Scotland) Ltd v Meiland* 1981 SLT (Notes) 72.

basis of her valuation of future losses. Her failure to do so will be founded upon'. A call is therefore,

> a warning to call the opponent's attention to the state of his averments, that he might have no reason afterwards to complain that he was taken by surprise, or that he understood that no greater specification was wanted.[34]

Of course, just because the defender (or the pursuer) says that further specification is required does not make it so. But a failure to answer a call might be interpreted as an implied admission that the person making the call is correct.[35] You must, however, be wary of sprinkling your pleadings with calls upon your opponent to supply further and better particulars: she might very well do precisely that, and thereby deprive you of decree of dismissal by converting a hopelessly irrelevant action into one of stunning relevancy.

As far as the order of the defender's pleas is concerned, we recommend the following:

1. Jurisdiction
2. Competency
3. Title to sue
4. *Forum non conveniens*
5. *Lis alibi pendens*
6. Relevancy (general)
7. Relevancy (particular averments)
8. Pleas on the merits of the pursuer's case
9. Pleas to substantive defences
10. Pleas regarding mode of proof
11. Pleas to quantum

---

[34] *Gordon v Davidson* (1864) 2 M 758 at 768 per the Lord Justice Clerk (Inglis).
[35] *Marine & Offshore (Scotland) Ltd v Robert Jack* [2017] CSOH 89, 2018 SCLR 183 at para 56 per Lord Bannatyne.

The pleas should be in the form of distinct legal propositions (e.g., 'In respect that the pursuer has no title to sue, the action should be dismissed'). However, in relation to some pleas it is the almost invariable practice to use an abbreviated form and simply say 'No jurisdiction' or 'No title to sue' or '*Forum non conveniens*' or '*Lis alibi pendens*'. This is strictly bad form, but it is probably too ingrained in practice for anything to be done about it. The practice should not, however, be extended further than it has already gone. You should certainly never abbreviate pleas to the competency or relevancy.

Finally, it is worth bearing in mind the following. If a preliminary plea is sustained (e.g. a plea to relevancy, specification, competency, jurisdiction, no title to sue, limitation), the action is dismissed, but it can be re-raised without being met by a plea of *res judicata*.[36] On the other hand, if the court sustains a plea on the merits (e.g., the pursuer's averments being unfounded in fact), even if of a dilatory or peremptory nature (e.g. prescription, *res judicata*), then decree of absolvitor is pronounced and the action cannot be re-raised.

Counterclaims

Before we finish this chapter on defences, we should mention a useful tool at the defender's disposal: the counterclaim. In short, the counterclaim procedure permits a defender who wishes to pursue a claim against the pursuer, arising out of the same set of circumstances as the pursuer's action against the defender, to do so in the same proceedings rather than by raising separate proceedings. Counterclaims are generally competent in both the sheriff court and the Court of Session. For ordinary causes in the sheriff court, chapter 19 of the Ordinary Cause Rules 1993 tells you when it is competent and what you need to do, and chapter 25 of the Rules of the Court of Session

---

[36] See Macphail, *Sheriff Court Practice*, ch 2, para 2.128 *et seq*.

1994 tells you what you need to do in that court. And as ever, Macphail's *Sheriff Court Practice* is a useful guide.[37]

For now, just remember the following:

- A counterclaim comes at the end of the defences and is headed 'COUNTERCLAIM FOR THE DEFENDER'.
- It requires a crave/conclusion.
- Instead of articles of condescendence, it proceeds by way of a statement of facts in numbered paragraphs.
- You can cross-refer and incorporate by reference any matter pled in the defences.
- The counterclaim needs its own pleas-in-law.

The pursuer then requires to answer the counterclaim, in the same manner as the defender has answered the writ.

---

[37] Ch 12, section IV.

CHAPTER FOUR

Adjustment and Amendment

Adjustment

In most types of proceedings, once the defences or answers have been lodged, there then follows what is known as the 'adjustment period'.[1] This is a period of usually around eight weeks wherein both parties can – and often must – respond to the averments of the other. It has been said that the

> object of adjustment is to make such alterations to the parties' averments and pleas-in-law as are necessary to ensure that when the record is closed the issues between the parties and the stand which each party is taking on these issues is properly focussed and may be readily understood from a reading of the pleadings.[2]

It is usually the pursuer who kicks things off and the pursuer should always adjust in response to the defences. Even if the defences are the boniest of skeletons, you will still want to adjust if only to take a plea to the relevancy of the defences and thus to pave the way for seeking decree *de plano*. Any plea to the relevancy of the defences should be stated at the

---

[1] This notably does not happen as of right in simple procedure actions or in judicial review procedure, albeit it normally does in the latter. And as noted in Chapter 5, the expectation in commercial actions is that the summons as lodged is the finished article or as close to the finished article as possible.

[2] Macphail, *Sheriff Court Practice*, ch 8, para 8.31, citing A G Walker, "Written Pleadings" (1963) 79 Sc L Rev 161 at 162–163.

end of the pursuer's original list of pleas and should not be inserted at the head of the list. This is a common error and, apart from being logically indefensible, involves the inconvenience of renumbering the original pleas. Again, give thought to whether in taking a plea to the relevancy you are seeking decree or whether it is intended that averments are excluded from probation.

If the defender has made substantive averments by way of explanation, you must respond to them in exactly the same way as a defender must answer the averments in the pursuer's condescendence. Make specific admissions, specific replies of 'Not known and not admitted', and end up with a general denial. These adjustments are added at the end of each article of condescendence and begin as follows: 'With reference to the defender's averments in answer, admitted that...'. They end with: '*Quoad ultra* the defender's averments in answer are denied except insofar as coinciding herewith'.

Do not on any account forget the general denial, since the pursuer, as much as the defender, is held to have admitted any averment by the other party which is within her knowledge and which she does not deny.[3] Be sure to adjust it in at the end of each article of condescendence. If the defender's averments make further explanations necessary on behalf of the pursuer, you should add them at the appropriate point, which is not necessarily at the end of the particular article of condescendence; the explanation may fit in more conveniently in the midst of averments made at an earlier stage. In addition, it should be remembered that the original pleadings may be revised, expanded upon or deleted as you think necessary. But be careful before doing a *volte-face* and changing the pursuer's position on a crucial matter of fact; while it may be perfectly explainable, the defender may take advantage of such a turnabout and ask the pursuer at proof how the change in position came to pass.

Once you have made your averments, the ball is then back in the court of the defender, who will adjust in response to

---

[3] *Central Motor Engineering Co v Galbraith* 1918 SC 755.

the pursuer's adjustments. This is done simply by adjusting the existing answers; you should certainly not confound matters further by saying 'With reference to the pursuer's averments in answer to the defender's averments in answer...'. If there is more than one defender, however, each defender may have to respond to the other defender's answers. If you are the first defender, this is done in the same way as the pursuer adjusts, i.e. 'With reference to the second defender's averments in answer ... *Quoad ultra* the second defender's averments in answer are denied except insofar as coinciding herewith'.

The pursuer may then adjust again. And so on ... and on ... (if you're lucky) and on ... (very lucky) until your luck runs out and the court refuses to grant any further continuation of the adjustment period and closes the record. Thereafter minutes of amendment are the order of the day.

But before we turn to those, a few points:

1. During the adjustment period, parties can adjust as of right[4] and unlike a minute of amendment, the leave of the court is not required. While the writ and defences are lodged with the court, adjustments are not. They are simply intimated to the other parties, and the pursuer will ultimately have the task of compiling a closed record for lodging.

2. Adjustments are done electronically and commence with the writ/defences being re-headed as follows: 'INITIAL WRIT (as adjusted as at X date)'/'DEFENCES (as adjusted as at X date)'. The adjustment must be obvious to the reader. At the very least, you must change the colour of the font and be sure that any deletions are scored through but still visible (i.e. do not just delete an averment so that it is lost to history). The easiest way to do this is to utilise 'track-changes'.

---

[4] As a general rule; although in commercial actions, structured adjustment is often allowed with, e.g. the pursuer adjusting first, then the defender, followed by a period of mutual adjustment.

3. If further adjustments are made, you do this on top of the first set of adjustments, so that both sets are visible. In that situation, the writ is headed 'INITIAL WRIT (as adjusted as at X date) (as further adjusted as at X date)'. Be sure that these further adjustments are in a different colour to the first set of adjustments. That can sometimes be tricky to accomplish if you are using track-changes. If technology gets the better of you and you cannot change the colour of the changes, put the further adjustments in bold.

4. The craves/conclusions and the designation of the parties can only be changed by amendment and cannot be the subject of adjustment.

5. So long as the action was raised timeously in the first case, a pursuer can make quite radical alterations to the case by adjustment, even if done so after the expiry of the time-limit.[5] This is in marked distinction to amendment, which is a procedure within the court's control.

6. Above all, bear in mind that adjustments should be about fine-tuning the pleadings rather than introducing brand new chapters. That is why it is so important to conduct your case analysis before the writ and defences are drafted. If you lodge only a barely relevant writ at the outset, or skeleton defences, which therefore require substantial adjustment, the other side will need time to investigate and respond to those adjustments which may well throw the action off course. You may well wonder: what's the harm in that? Well, all we can say is that it is most unwise to rely upon the court to grant extension after extension to the adjustment period.

Amendment

We can deal with amendment briefly because we are concerned here only with how to plead amendments rather than

---

[5] See *Coyle v National Coal Board* 1959 SLT 114; *Sellars v IMI Yorkshire Imperial Ltd* 1986 SC 235; *Cowan v Lanarkshire Housing Association* [2020] CSIH 26. 2020 SLT 663.

with when they are competent (or more importantly, incompetent) and the somewhat convoluted rules of procedure.[6] At this stage, you need know little more than these five points:

1. After the record has closed, the only way to alter the pleadings is by way of minute of amendment, and the pleadings can in principle be amended at any time – including during, and after, a debate, proof or appeal – up and until the final judgment is issued. Pretty much any aspect of the pleadings can be changed by amendment, including adding in new pursuers or new defenders/a third party.

2. With the exception of amending the sum sued for in a sheriff court writ before the record has closed,[7] amendment is *always* at the discretion of the court and you have no 'right' to amend. If someone suggests that something can 'just be amended in later', look at them with concern and respond: 'you hope'.[8]

3. For there to be even a chance of amending the pleadings, the proposed amendment must (obviously) be competent, and the court must be satisfied that the amendment is necessary for the purpose of determining the real question in controversy between the parties.[9] Even so, the court must also be satisfied that it is in the interests of justice to allow the amendment.[10] The court will take account of the stage the action is at, whether the amendment could have been made sooner, the nature of the amendment, any prejudice to the other party and what conditions (e.g. expenses) ought to be imposed.[11]

---

[6] Amendment procedure is dealt with in a standalone chapter in, you've guessed it, Macphail, *Sheriff Court Practice*, ch 10. See also OCR ch 18; and RCS ch 24.

[7] OCR r 18.1.

[8] Or, if in the commercial court, 'aye, right' may be more apt.

[9] OCR r 18.2(2)(a); RCS r 24.1(2)(a).

[10] *Thomson v Glasgow Corporation* 1962 SC (HL) 36.

[11] Macphail, *Sheriff Court Practice*, ch 10, para 10.14.

4. The court will not normally allow the pursuer to substitute the right defender for the wrong defender, to change the basis of its case or otherwise to cure a radical incompetence after the expiry of a time-limit.[12] Simply altering the formulation of the existing claim is different to, and will be treated with more sympathy than, adding in an entirely new ground of liability after a time-limit has expired.[13] In most cases, it is ultimately a matter for the discretion of the court, of particular relevance in respect of a limitation period in a personal injuries action.[14]

5. Amendment is almost always accompanied by an award of expenses against the amending party. Those expenses are likely to include the other side's expenses in answering the minute of amendment. If the pleadings are amended close to the diet of proof and if the proof is discharged as a result, the amending party should be prepared to meet the expenses occasioned by the discharge too.

So how do you amend? Leaving aside those straightforward, technical amendments which can be and normally are made orally at the bar of the court, you will need to draft a minute of amendment. Be warned: this can be a painful exercise – depending on the size of the record – both for the party amending and for the party responding.

You start by identifying what it is you would like to (or feel that you have to) add to your pleadings. It may be that you have just come across essential new information or that you have a wake-up-in-a-cold-sweat moment and realise that you have pled the wrong ground of fault. Regardless, once you have it clear in your head what you need to plead, you next must identify where in the pleadings as they stand currently

---

[12] *Pompa's Trustees v Magistrates of Edinburgh* 1942 SC 119 at 125 per the Lord Justice Clerk (Cooper). See also *Hynd v West Fife Co-operative Ltd* 1980 SLT 41; cf. *Perth and Kinross Council v Scottish Water Ltd* [2016] CSIH 83, 2016 SLT 1251.

[13] See also *Sellars v IMI Yorkshire Imperial Ltd* 1985 SC 235.

[14] Prescription and Limitation (Scotland) Act 1973, s 19A.

these new averments ought to be inserted. That does not mean just identifying the particular article of condescendence or page number of the record (although you must do both of these things), but identifying the very sentence which requires to be amended or the sentence after which you require to add the new averment.

It will be easier to see an example:

JOHNSTON for the pursuer craves the court to allow the closed record to be opened up and amended as follows:

(1) In article four of condescendence, at the top of page 29, delete the sentence commencing 'In the circumstances...' and substitute it with the following:
     'Those failures caused or materially contributed to the assault on the pursuer.'
(2) In article five of condescendence, at the end of page 34, after the sentence ending '...not responsive to treatment.', insert the following:
     'The pursuer is permanently unfit to work.'

And of new to close to record.

The defender will then lodge answers to the minute of amendment, which start like this:

SCULLION for the defender craves the court to allow the minute of amendment for the pursuer, number   of process, to be answered as follows:

It is then just the same process as the pursuer has undertaken, substituting 'article four...' with 'answer 4', and so on.

But rather than worrying about any particular form of wording, the important thing is to keep the objective in mind. That is to allow the court, when deciding whether or not to allow the pleadings to be amended, to take hold of the record in the one hand and the minute of amendment and answers in the other, and work out precisely what averments parties wish to add and to delete. Indeed, you may even wish to go the extra mile and mark up the pleadings with the proposed amendment to make it easier for the sheriff to follow what is being proposed. So long as you have done what you can to ensure that everyone knows what you are proposing to amend, and followed the relevant rules of court for the procedure, all will – or should be – well.

CHAPTER FIVE

Special Causes

Personal injuries actions

Introduction

Special rules apply to most personal injuries actions[1] in both the sheriff court and the Court of Session. These are contained in chapter 36 of the Sheriff Court Ordinary Cause Rules, and chapter 43 of the Rules of the Court of Session. These rules require a different approach or culture to be taken to personal injury actions, and, in particular, they mandate a more relaxed approach to pleading.[2] We will come back to how to plead the meat of your writ below, but in summary, the initial writ or summons must be in the prescribed form,[3] to which is annexed a *brief* statement containing averments in numbered paragraphs relating *only* to those facts *necessary* (emphasis added) to establish the claim;[4] and the names of every medical practitioner from whom, and every hospital or other institution in which, the pursuer (or in an action in respect of the death of a person, the deceased) received treatment for the personal injuries.[5] The prescribed forms[6] contain an instance and craves/conclusions in the usual way. However, the statement of claim is

---

[1] Other than those which fall within chapter 36A of the OCR, and chapter 42A of the RCS.

[2] *Higgins v DHL International* (UK) Ltd 2003 SLT 1301 at para 28 per Lady Paton.

[3] RCS r 43.2(1); OCR r 36.B1(1).

[4] RCS r 43.2(1)(a); OCR r 36.B1(a).

[5] RCS r 43.2(1)(b); OCR r 36.B1(b).

[6] Form 43.2-A for the Court of Session; form P1 for the sheriff court.

considerably abbreviated in comparison with the condescend-ence in traditional pleadings, and there are no pleas-in-law.

So far, so straightforward you might think. But not every personal injuries action is governed by the chapter 36, or 43, procedure, and there are inevitably several pitfalls for you to fall into (or trip over) along the way. So, before raising any personal injuries action, or beginning to draft any writ, as ever, you should think. In particular, (at least) ask yourself the fol-lowing questions.

Will the action be a 'personal injuries action'?

Usually, this will be obvious. The client sitting opposite you with his leg in plaster because he fell into a hole in the pave-ment, or who nearly died on the operating table due to the negligence of her surgeon, has clearly sustained a personal injury. But what of the client who is suffering from a disease brought about by the inhalation of a noxious substance, or from **PTSD** caused by bullying at work? They, too, are suffer-ing from personal injuries, which are defined as including 'any disease or impairment, whether physical or mental'.[7] Further, the grieving relative who wants to sue the person responsible for the death of a loved one will also be pursuing a personal injuries action, which is, according to the rules, 'an action of damages for, or arising from, personal injuries or death of a person from personal injuries'.[8]

A trickier situation is where your client is only consulting you because they want to sue their previous, hopelessly inept, solicitor, who failed to raise an action within the triennium, and the court declined to grant equitable relief.[9] You might think that such an action ought to be able to take advantage of the rules, because many of the issues in the case will be iden-tical to those which would have arisen in the original action had it been raised in time, such as the averments of fault, and

---

[7] RCS r 43.1(2); OCR r 36.A1(3).
[8] RCS r 43.1(2); OCR r 36.A1(2).
[9] Under section 19A of the Prescription and Limitation (Scotland) Act 1973.

the approach to quantification of damages. You might also think that support for that view is gained from the definition, since although an action against the solicitors would not be an action *for* personal injuries, it is, at least arguably, one which arises *from* personal injuries. In *Tudhope v Park*,[10] an action for damages for professional negligence in failing to raise an action within the triennium was allowed to be registered under chapter 43, albeit the Lord Ordinary surmised that it would likely be removed from that procedure following the lodging of defences, being manifestly unsuitable for it. However, at a later stage in that action, a different Lord Ordinary appointed the action to proceed as an ordinary action, on the basis that it was not, after all, one which fell within chapter 43: it arose from alleged professional negligence and not from personal injuries.[11] So, in drafting a professional negligence action arising from a botched personal injuries one, unless you want to argue that the second Lord Ordinary in *Tudhope* was wrong, you should not use the abbreviated form of pleading provided for by the rules.

When will the triennium expire?

This is arguably the most important question of them all. Do not be that soon-to-be-sued solicitor in the last example. Find out when your client's injury happened, or when her operation was, or when they first began to experience symptoms. If in doubt about when time-bar began to run, opt for the earliest date when it might conceivably run out, and then diarise it. Don't diarise only that date, but diarise suitable warnings six months, three months, two months, one month, one week, before that date. That all said, if your client comes through your door on a Monday, and the triennium is about to expire on the Thursday, the normal pleading niceties (as in any situation where a claim is about to prescribe or time-bar) go out of the window and the priority is to get a writ, any writ, into

---

[10] 2003 SLT 1305.
[11] 2004 SLT 783.

court, served on the defender, and then move to sist the action while more leisurely investigations are carried out.

How much is the claim worth?

Logically, this is probably the next question you should ask, if only because it has a bearing on the question relating to the choice of *forum*. At this stage, you are not reaching a final valuation of your client's claim (although if you have engaged in pre-action correspondence as you ought to have done, you should have a reasonable idea of its likely true value). All you are really doing in addressing this question is asking whether the claim is likely worth more, or less, than £100,000, the limit of the privative jurisdiction of the sheriff court.

At the other end of the spectrum, you will also need to decide whether the claim is likely worth more or less than £25,000, because…

Does the pre-action protocol apply?

…a pre-action protocol applies to all claims arising on or after 28 November 2016 where the reasonably estimated value of the claim is no more than £25,000, excepting claims arising from alleged clinical or professional negligence[12] or that take the form of a disease.[13] Where the protocol does apply you must follow it; otherwise your client runs the risk of being penalised in expenses or being forced by the court to follow the protocol after an action has been raised.[14]

Where should I raise the action?

We refer to what we say above at pages 18 to 21. The main point for present purposes is that you will have a choice of

---

[12] Although, as we have seen, these are not personal injuries actions in any event.

[13] Act of Sederunt (Sheriff Court Rules Amendment) (Personal Injury Pre-Action Protocol) 2016.

[14] OCR ch 3A.2 and 3A.3; see also ch 4A, which applies to summary cause actions.

potentially three (or more) courts, depending on the value of the claim, the place of the accident and the domicile of the defender: the Court of Session, the Sheriff Personal Injury Court or the local sheriff court(s) which have jurisdiction. Just remember that if you wish to preserve the right to a jury trial in a sheriff court action, the action must be raised in the Sheriff Personal Injury Court.

The craves/conclusions

However much you think the claim is worth, in personal injuries actions it is common to allow some margin for error in selecting the sum sued for, since the normal rule applies that the court cannot grant decree for more than the sum craved or concluded for. Although the sum sued for can be increased as of right during the adjustment period, and by amendment with leave of the court after that, it is good practice to sue for a sum greater than the sum which will probably be awarded.

In some cases, for example where your client is suffering from pleural plaques and it is uncertain whether or not a more serious condition may develop, you may have the option of suing for provisional damages. Section 12(2)(a) of the Administration of Justice Act 1982 makes it competent to include a crave or conclusion for provisional damages in addition to a crave or conclusion for full and final damages. Where you do that, your crave or conclusion should make clear that these remedies are sought in the alternative.

Finally, it is normal to crave interest from a date earlier than the date of decree although strictly unnecessary to do so.[15]

The instance – who are the parties?

As in any other action, the pursuer must be named and designed in the instance. However, if the action is one arising out of sexual abuse, or otherwise involves sensitive issues, you will need to consider whether to apply for the court by motion

---

[15] *Orr v Metcalfe* 1973 SLT 133, applying section 1A of the Interest on Damages (Scotland) Act 1958.

for an order that the pursuer be anonymised in all documents issued by the court, and for an order in terms of section 11 of the Contempt of Court Act 1981. In that case, your client's name should appear in the writ or summons presented to the court, but your motion for anonymisation should be presented to the court as soon as possible, to ensure that the name does not subsequently appear in the rolls of court or the like.

In an action arising out of a death,[16] you may be acting for more than one member of the deceased's family. That is one situation where you are able to have multiple pursuers in a personal injuries action.[17] You will need a separate crave or conclusion for each. Where a relative is also the executor, there should be a separate conclusion or crave for the sum due to him or her in each capacity. Where the same person sues on behalf of more than one child, there should be a separate conclusion or crave for each.

However, you may not have instructions from all members of the deceased's family entitled to bring a claim. In that case, you will need to include in your crave, or conclusion, a request for warrant to intimate to all 'connected persons'. A connected person is a person, not being a party to the action, who has title to sue the defender in respect of the personal injuries from which a deceased died or in respect of his death. They are: (a) the executor(s) and (b) relatives, as defined in the Damages (Scotland) Act 2011. It follows that in a death case, you must aver, either, that there are no connected persons; or that there are connected persons, being the persons specified in the warrant for intimation; or that there are connected persons but that intimation should be dispensed with on the ground that their names or whereabouts are not known to the pursuer and cannot reasonably be ascertained; or such persons are unlikely to be awarded more than the sum of £200 each.[18] Note that

---

[16] That is, an action in which damages are claimed (a) in respect of injuries from which the deceased died; or (b) in respect of the death of the deceased.

[17] See also p 27.

[18] RCS r 43.14(2).

intimation cannot be dispensed with on any other ground. In a recent case presented to the Court of Session, the mother of a deceased child sought to dispense with intimation to the father on the grounds that he had never been part of the child's life, and she did not wish him to pursue a claim in her action, but dispensation on that ground was refused.

As for the correct identity of the defender, hopefully any issues will have been identified and resolved in pre-litigation correspondence, at least where the pre-action protocol has been invoked and followed, and possibly in cases falling out-with the protocol, in that the defender's insurers or solicitor should have confirmed whether liability on the part of the defender is admitted or not, and if not admitted, on what grounds. However, in a personal injuries action arising out of an accident at work, remember to work out who the employer is. Most commonly in an action arising out of a road traffic accident, or occasionally in certain other situations, you may wish to convene the insurers of the wrongdoer as an additional (or as the sole) defender,[19] although beware the dangers of doing so on too cavalier a basis: *Harvie* v *Avrameeouru and Others*.[20]

Next, a couple of wrinkles. Particularly in industrial disease cases, where your client was employed by a limited company which has ceased to trade, you should check with Companies House whether the company is still in existence or whether it has been dissolved. If the latter, before you can raise a personal injuries action, you will need to petition the court to have the company restored to the register: an action cannot competently be raised against a non-existent person (although you would be surprised at how often restoration petitions are presented in relation to companies against which an action has already been raised). On a related theme, if the defender company has

---

[19] By virtue of Regulation 3 of the European Communities (Rights against Insurers) Regulations 2002 as amended by the Motor Vehicles (Compulsory Insurance and Rights Against Insurers) (Amendment) (EU Exit) Regulations 2020; or the Third Parties (Rights against Insurers) Act 2010.

[20] [2023] SC EDIN 41.

been wound up by the court, and is in liquidation, leave of the court will be needed before an action can be raised.[21] In either case, of course, there should be insurers in place, on whom any petition should be served (or at least, to whom intimation should be given).

Should you move the court to disapply chapter 36/43?

The 'standard' procedure provided for by chapters 36 and 43 is not intended to cover every personal injuries action: in particular it is not suitable for actions of particular complexity, which are more suitable for case management. Most personal injuries actions based on alleged clinical negligence proceed as ordinary actions, with traditional pleading , but governed by chapter 36A OCR or chapter 42A RCS. If you intend to go down that route, you must draft a summons or initial writ in traditional form (with reasonably detailed pleadings, and pleas-in-law) and include a draft interlocutor in the prescribed form seeking authority to raise the action.[22] This will then be presented to a Lord Ordinary or sheriff, as the case may be, who will either grant it or assign a hearing for both parties to be heard. For the order to be granted, the judge must consider the likely complexity of the action and be satisfied that the efficient determination of the action will be served by the action proceeding as a chapter 36A or chapter 42A action, which, in a clinical negligence case, will almost invariably be the case, but make sure that your pleadings adequately demonstrate the complexity involved. It is also open to a party to apply to have an action withdrawn from chapter 43 procedure within 28 days of the lodging of defences, which the court may grant if there are exceptional reasons for doing so, having regard, among other things, to the likely need for detailed pleadings.[23]

---

[21] Insolvency Act 1986, s 130(3).

[22] OCR r 36.C1(2); RCS r 43.1A(2).

[23] OCR r 36, F1; RCS r 43.5.

How to draft the condescendence in a chapter 36/43 action

Let us assume, finally, that you have asked and answered all of the foregoing questions. You have decided which court to raise your action in, you have valued the claim and decided how much to sue for, and you have identified the defender, which still exists. You have complied with the pre-action protocol, but the defender's insurers are stubbornly refusing to settle. The action is not complex enough to justify it being taken out of chapter 36 (or 43). How do you next go about drafting the condescendence itself, bearing in mind the injunction in the rules that pleadings be brief and should contain only those facts necessary to establish the claim? How brief can you afford to be, bearing in mind that you must always give fair notice of your claim to the defender?

Before attempting to answer that question, it is useful to make a brief foray into history, to understand how we got to where we are today, and the mischief that the current rules were intended to eradicate. The Court of Session Rules (on which the sheriff court rules are based) are a product of Lord Coulsfield's Working Party on Court of Session Procedure. In its first report, published in 2000,[24] it observed that:

> the present form of pleadings is too elaborate and cumbersome, and occupies too much time at the start of a litigation, time which is often really wasted.

The report then contains a useful historical summary of how the Scottish system of pleading evolved, noting that the criticisms which were being advanced in the mid-19th century were that written pleadings were diffuse, mingled averments of fact and argument in such a way as to make it difficult to see what a party's case was,[25] and they were drawn with a view

---

[24] Available at https://www.scotcourts.gov.uk/media/mstniio2/lord -coulsfield-report-by-working-party-on-cos-procedure.pdf.

[25] Plus ça change, you might say, on reading the trenchant comments of Lady Dorrian and Sheriff Principal Anwar, above.

to assisting the court to decide cases without entering into any factual enquiry (you may raise an eyebrow, but the same could be said of many petitions which call before the Court of Session today). To combat those difficulties, the present system developed from about 1850, when the form of summons was amended more or less to that used in ordinary actions to the present day. [26] While, as we have seen, writers such as Lees advocated simple pleadings, setting forth only those facts necessary for proof of a party's case, over time pleadings went from being 'remarkably brief' to being over-elaborate. The Working Party ascribed this to a number of factors, including an (over) anxiety about giving the other party fair notice of one's case and a fear of not being allowed to lead evidence on a crucial fact if it had not been pled; both, no doubt, driven by the culture in the courts in the mid-20th century, when 'highly technical' objections, otherwise known as nit-picking pleading points, were routinely taken at debate.

All of this led the Working Party to conclude that more was required than simply to express a general aspiration that pleadings should be short and simple. That had been tried by Lees and others and had simply not worked. It thought that the only pleading that was required in relation to liability was the:

> briefest description of the events on which the claim is based, together with a brief indication of the ground of fault alleged, and a specific reference to any statutory provision which may be founded on.

The Working Party acknowledged that guidance both to the parties and to the bench as to what degree of specification was necessary would be helpful, and provided some suggested terse (and, it must be acknowledged, fairly radical) styles in an appendix. By way of example, how is this for a pithy statement of facts:

---

[26] See the Court of Session Act 1850.

The pursuer was employed by the defenders as a woodworker at their premises at _____. On _____ he was working at a circular saw and was injured by coming in to contact with the saw blade, which was unguarded.

Or:

On _____ at _____ pm the pursuer was crossing _____ Road when he was struck and knocked down by a car driven by the defender's employee _____ in the course of his employment.

These proposals certainly did what they said on the tin, in that they were as brief as brief could be – certainly, if adopted, that would have resulted in a radically different approach to written pleading in personal injuries actions. However, they were too radical for the Court of Session Rules Council, which endorsed views which had been expressed to it that the Working Party's proposal was not workable, perhaps on the IAB principle,[27] or maybe it was simply felt that the Working Party had gone too far in the opposite direction by requiring virtually no specification whatsoever of the details of how an accident had happened. A representative group of the Working Party was asked to re-examine the original proposals, which resulted in a Supplementary Report in 2003.[28] Broadly speaking, the Working Party remained of the view that pleadings in personal injury actions were, as a rule, too elaborate and technical and that what was required was pleadings which were 'short and excluded stylistic phrases and ritual incantations'. It proposed that pleadings should be couched in such a way as to require individual answers to individual statements of fact. Finally, the Working Party provided three further examples, taken from real cases, of how pleadings might be made shorter and

---

[27] 'It's aye been' – a traditionally Scottish approach, meaning, 'we don't know why we do it this way but we always have so there is no need to change it'.

[28] Available at https://www.scotcourts.gov.uk/media/fwsedkti/lord -coulsfield-supplementary-report-by-working-party.pdf.

simpler in line with their recommended approach.[29] Broadly speaking the two key themes which can be gleaned from these examples are the use of short paragraphs or sub-paragraphs, each consisting of a single sentence, making it much easier for individual averments to be admitted or denied; and (repeating a theme from the Working Party's original report) an expectation that details of the pursuer's loss would be given in the statement of valuation of claim, rather than in the pleadings themselves, resulting in very brief averments of loss.

This Report did find favour and new Court of Session rules governing personal injury actions were introduced from 1 April 2003, with the sheriff court following suit on 2 November 2009.

It is a moot point as to whether, more than 20 years after the current rules were introduced into the Court of Session, the aim of brevity in pleadings has been universally achieved. Certainly, debates are very much the exception, and to that extent the rules have proved to be a success. Such case law as there is makes clear that cases which previously may have failed to meet the traditional tests of relevancy and specification will now be allowed to proceed to proof, even where it is difficult for the court to identify factual averments which would entitle the pursuer to lead evidence establishing a basis for (for example) the contention that the defenders ought reasonably to have foreseen that the pursuer would be likely to suffer injury in the circumstances.[30] In other words, the court, more often than not, is likely to take the view that it cannot decide, before hearing evidence, whether the facts averred are sufficient to support the legal conclusion which the pursuer requires for success.[31]

---

[29] Ibid.

[30] See for example *Higgins v DHL International (UK) Ltd*; *Hamilton v Seamark Systems Ltd* 2004 SC 543; *Fenwick v Dundas* [2022] CSOH 62, 2022 SLT 1114.

[31] *Hamilton v Seamark Systems*, per Lady Paton, citing *Moore v Stephen & Sons* 1954 SC 331 at 335.

All of this provides some comfort to the would-be personal injuries pleader. It is unlikely that an action will be dismissed as so lacking in specification as to disentitle you to a proof.

However, that may provide scant comfort to you when faced with the task of drafting an initial writ or summons since pleadings which clear that hurdle may nonetheless be so lacking in specification as to be unsuitable for jury trial[32] or lead to problems at proof should objection be taken to a particular line of evidence. There will often be a fine line between averring only those bare facts necessary to establish the claim, and failing to give fair notice to the defender of what the pursuer's case is.

So, how are you to successfully tread that line? We suggest that what you are aiming for is something between the minimalist examples given by the Working Party in its first report, and the mindless stream of consciousness pleading running to page after page after page, which sometimes still graces our courts. The first place to look for guidance is the style statement in the prescribed form, which has six numbered paragraphs, the first three of which contain formal averments regarding the parties' designation and jurisdiction. The fourth paragraph is to 'contain a brief statement of the facts necessary to establish the claim', but that gives no guidance as to what, in any particular case, those facts should be. The fifth paragraph is to set out the injuries suffered and the heads of claim and should include the hospitals or other institutions in which the pursuer or deceased received treatment, and the sixth should state whether the claim is based on fault at common law or breach of statutory duty – if the latter, the provision or provisions require to be stated.

As for what should go into that fourth paragraph, the same advice as appears throughout this book applies: think! What *are* the facts *necessary* to establish the claim? Aver those facts. Are there any other facts about which you might wish to lead evidence? If so, then aver those too. For example, in a road

---

[32] As was the case in *Higgins*, although jury trials are relatively rare these days.

traffic accident caused by the defender driving on to the pursuer's side of the road, it would be sufficient to aver that bare fact. If the defender was subsequently convicted of dangerous driving, and you wish to lead evidence of that conviction, as you would be entitled to do, then it would be prudent to make an averment about it.

It is instructive to examine one of the suggested examples given by the Working Party (adapting it in line with the prescribed forms, and modifying the grammar).

Statement of Claim

1. The pursuer was born on 30 January 1967.

2. The defender is a company incorporated under the Companies Acts and has a place of business at the address in the instance.

3. The court has jurisdiction to hear this claim against the defender because the harmful event giving rise to the claim occurred in Scotland.

4A. On 3 June 1998 the pursuer was a bus assembler employed by the defender.

4B. On said date the pursuer was working on the Olympian Line fitting an anti-roll bar to a bus, which consisted of a rod 5cm (2 inches) in diameter and about 304cm (ten feet) in length in a solid metal construction.

4C. A rod was fitted across the width of a bus around 91cm (three feet) from ground height.

4D. This was not the pursuer's normal job as the employee who did the job, Thomas Ferguson, was absent for a week.

4E. The pursuer was carrying out the job as he had seen Mr Ferguson doing it and had not been otherwise trained or instructed in the job.

4F. To fit the rod the pursuer exerted force from a crouching position on one knee placing the end of the rod onto the front of the chassis where it was bolted.

4G. The pursuer used a pinch bar held in his left hand to wedge the end of the rod in the proper place for connection to the chassis.

4H. There was no mechanical device to send to the rod or to guide it to where it was fitted.

4I. The pursuer was locating the rod, when the pinch bar jammed and suddenly released, and released the rod with the pinch bar hitting the pursuer on his right shin and the rod on his right knee.

4J. There was no harness provided to support the rod while being located.

4K. Following the accident the defenders provided no alternative type of pinch wear and instructed operators as to the correct method of construction.

5A. The pursuer's injury:

(i) Damaged anterior cruciate ligament bucket handle tear of the cartilage of the right knee.

(ii) Adjustment disorder with mixed anxiety and depressed mood.

5B. Treated by:

(i) [GP details].

(ii) Crosshouse Hospital, Kilmarnock.

5C. Heads of claim

(i) Solatium

(ii) Earnings lost till June 2000.

(iii) Earnings loss from employment he would have obtained.

(iv) Future earnings loss or, failing which, loss of employability on the open labour market.

(v) Cost of travelling for medical treatment.

(vi) Prescription costs.

(vii) Service provided by pursuer which he can no longer perform for his parents since the year 2000.

(viii) Services the pursuer is unable to carry out by way of home decoration, gardening and car maintenance.

6A. The defenders failed to take reasonable care for the safety of the pursuer and exposed him to risk of injury by devising a safe system of work.

6B. The defenders failed to take reasonable care to provide safe and adequate plant and equipment.

6C. The defenders were in breach of the following statutory duties:

(i) Regulation 13 of the Workplace (Health, Safety and Welfare) Regulations 1992;

(ii) Regulation 5 of the Provisions and Use of Work Equipment Regulations 1992;

(iii) Regulation 20 of the Provisions and Use of Work Equipment Regulations 1992.

It is fair to say that in the 20 years or so since the Working Party came up with that example, pleadings have not developed in line with their suggested approach. The idea of splitting the statement of facts necessary to establish the claim into lettered sub-paragraphs, each consisting of a single sentence, is not to everyone's taste but is arguably preferable to stream of consciousness pleading, often extending to several pages without so much as a pause for breath.

At the end of the day, you will need to work out your own style. Remember the advice given earlier. Think before putting pen to paper. Whether you adopt the style of one sentence to a paragraph or not, short, snappy sentences are better than long rambling ones. Try to aver only those facts essential for proof of your client's claim. If you intend to lead evidence of other facts, give the defender fair notice by making averments of those facts too. Only the briefest averments of loss are necessary, as there the devil is in the detail of the statement of valuation of claim. Only broad averments of breach of duty are required. There are no pleas-in-law.

Defences

Perhaps paradoxically, the rules do not contain any guidance as to the form defences in personal injuries actions should take. Strictly speaking, rule 18.1 (which requires pleas-in-law) applies but Practice Note no 3 of 2004 states that defences must not contain pleas-in-law. Defenders who wish to include in their pleadings an outline of their propositions in law should do so by inserting a brief summary of those propositions in the last answer of the defences. As with all pleadings, the duty of candour exists at all times, to serve both the court and the parties.[33] Blanket denials or skeleton defences are not an acceptable starting point.[34]

Chapter 36A / 42A actions
If chapter 36 or 43 has been disapplied, then depending on whether you are in the sheriff court or the Court of Session,

---

[33] PN No 2 of 2014.
[34] Subject to what is said in Chapter 3.

your action will be governed by chapter 36A or 42A and will proceed as an ordinary action. No special rules of pleading apply to those, and you should, therefore, adopt the traditional approach dealt with in Chapter 2 of this book.

Commercial actions

Why raise an action as a commercial action?

If your client is involved in a commercial dispute, it will almost certainly make sense, if you can, to raise it as a commercial action for a variety of reasons, not least that the procedure in these is quicker and more flexible than in an ordinary action; your case will also be dealt with by a sheriff or judge with experience and expertise in commercial matters, commercial actions are pro-actively case managed, and finally, relevant for present purposes, concise pleading is the order of the day.

Do you need a letter before action?

Except in cases of extreme urgency – for example, where an interim interdict is needed to prevent your client's trade secrets from being passed to a competitor by a disgruntled former employee who is threatening to do just that – you have one advantage when it comes to drafting a summons or initial writ in a commercial action, or at least, when you intend to litigate in either the commercial court of the Court of Session, or in a sheriff court which has a commercial roll,[35] and that is time, and in particular, time to think. You will get short shrift in

---

[35] At the time of writing: Glasgow, Edinburgh, Aberdeen, Inverness, Jedburgh, Selkirk, the Tayside courts (Dundee, Forfar and Perth), Hamilton and Airdrie Sheriff Courts. Commercial actions emanating from Aberdeen, Peterhead and Banff sheriff court districts will be accepted at Aberdeen. Commercial actions emanating from Inverness, Elgin, Fort William, Portree, Stornoway, Lochmaddy, Tain and Wick sheriff court districts may all be raised at Inverness. Cases emanating from Lerwick and Kirkwall sheriff court districts may be raised in Aberdeen Sheriff Court or Inverness Sheriff Court.

any commercial court (and risk an award of expenses being awarded against your client) if you roll up at the first preliminary hearing, with a diffuse and rambling writ, without first having engaged in the relevant pre-action protocol, the purpose of which is to focus the dispute on the issues which are truly contentious and to present the court with an 'oven-ready' dispute upon which it can adjudicate (well, that's the theory, anyway).

So, the first thing you should do when accepting instructions in a commercial dispute is not to dust down your styles library but to formulate your client's claim in a letter before action. If nothing else, this has the merit (or should do) of forcing you to think about your client's claim and what is the legal basis of it, as well as identifying what documents support it (such as, depending on the nature of the claim, a lease, share purchase agreement or a building contract). Of course, not every letter before action receives a response, but sometimes you will receive a reasoned response, perhaps containing a powerful defence to your client's claim causing you to have a rapid re-think about the strength of your client's claim, perhaps not. Some disputes will settle at this stage, but assume that the correspondence makes clear that the defender is completely intransigent and that there is as much chance of the other side agreeing to pay your client anything approaching a reasonable sum as there is of a snowball surviving in Hades, or the Scottish football team qualifying for the knock-out stages of a major tournament,[36] and that you conclude that there is after all no alternative to raising a court action: what then?

Where to litigate?
The first thing you will have to decide, as with any litigation, is *where* to litigate. If your client's claim is worth £100,000 or less, of course, there will be no choice: you must litigate in the sheriff court. But if it is worth more than that, you will have the option of raising an action in the Court of Session. If you must,

---

[36] Statistically, the snowball's odds of survival are greater.

or choose to, litigate in the sheriff court, your next decision will be: which one? Can you establish jurisdiction in a sheriff court which has a commercial court? Most sheriffdoms (the exception being North Strathclyde) have at least one commercial court.[37]

Is the dispute a commercial dispute?

The next thing to check, if you are considering raising a commercial action, is whether the action does indeed involve a commercial dispute. It is usually obvious – two multinational companies at loggerheads over the meaning of a distribution contract, or who have fallen out over a building contract, are clearly engaged in a commercial dispute. But sometimes, it is less clear cut. What if your client has commissioned a house to be built for him and his family to live in, and wants to sue the builder? Or contends that the legal advice she received from her previous lawyers was negligent and wishes to sue them for damages? Are they embroiled in commercial disputes? The practice note contains a list of the most common types of commercial dispute[38] but generally the commercial court, certainly in the Court of Session, takes a broad view as to what is a commercial dispute, and if both parties label the dispute as a commercial one, then unless it is clearly not of a commercial hue, the court is likely to accept it as such.

Drafting a summons/initial writ

The guiding principle when drafting pleadings in a commercial action is that the procedure is intended to provide an efficient and flexible means of resolving disputes of a commercial or business nature. The principal purpose, and over-riding requirement, of the pleadings is to give fair notice of the essential elements of the case to the court and to the other parties

---

[37] See n 35.
[38] PN 1 of 2017, para 2.

to the action.[39] Thus, pleadings in traditional form are not normally required or encouraged in a commercial action.[40] As Lord President Carloway reminded parties in *Marine & Offshore (Scotland) Ltd v Hill*,[41] the rules applicable to averments in an ordinary action do not normally apply with the same rigour in a commercial one; lengthy narrative is to be avoided. In that case, the pleadings of both parties were criticised as 'voluminous', running to 34 closely line spaced pages, and the lengthy narrative provided by the pursuer was said to '[serve] largely to obscure rather than clarify the facts' and to give rise to a 'narrative mist'.[42] Sadly, the pleadings in that case are by no means atypical, and pleaders in commercial actions often regrettably err on the side of prolixity.

The remainder of this section is devoted to helping you to avoid falling into that error. By the time you come to draft the initial writ or summons, the dispute should already have crystallised: it should be obvious what the issues are and what facts you must aver and prove in order to establish your client's case. This should help you to avoid unnecessary verbiage in your writ. Remember above all that the principle underlying the commercial court is to get to the heart of the dispute rather than to focus on traditional and perhaps arcane rules of pleading.

You still do need a conclusion, in traditional form, and to specify who the parties are.[43] The court will not look kindly on

---

[39] See, e.g. Sheriffdom of South Strathclyde, Dumfries and Galloway Practice Note No 1 of 2022; Sheriffdom of Grampian Highland and Islands Practice Note No 1 of 2018; Court of Session Practice Note No 1 of 2017.

[40] See, e.g. PN No 1 of 2017, para 13(a). The other Practice Notes are to similar effect.

[41] [2018] CSIH 9, 2018 SLT 239.

[42] At paras 17–18 per the Lord President (Carloway).

[43] RCS r 47.3(2) provides that the summons in a commercial action *shall* (a) specify, in the form of conclusions, the orders sought; and (b) identify the parties to the action and the transaction or dispute from which the action arises.

a summons or initial writ which does not set out what remedy the pursuer seeks, or from whom. However, after that, the rule book, in theory at least, pretty much goes out the window and, in the words of the song, anything goes. One example given in the Practice Notes[44] is that where it is sought to obtain from the court a decision only on the construction of a document, it is permissible for the summons to contain an appropriate conclusion without annexing articles of condescendence or pleas-in-law. The conclusion should specify the document the construction of which is in dispute and the construction contended for. It is fair to say that writs and summons which follow that guidance have been about as rare as hen's teeth – it is thought that there was once a sighting, many years ago – but the guidance is there. If you have a case where the only issue is whether a document means A or B, have the courage to adopt that approach. If challenged, point to the Practice Note!

A less extreme example is where the issue between the parties turns on a point of law. The summons or initial writ may contain a brief summary of the pursuer's argument including, if necessary, reference to authority:[45] heresy in an ordinary action, but permissible in the commercial court.

However, most commercial actions involve at least some measure of dispute on the facts, and some averment of facts will be necessary. The challenge here is to do that in a way which gives fair notice to the other side, without indulging in 'narrative mist' or, as it is otherwise known, the sort of pleading which is often seen in a traditional ordinary action. One obvious means of doing that is by reference to other documentation. Where the pursuer's position on any matter is contained in another document, such as a Scott Schedule or the conclusions of an expert report, it is permissible to adopt the document, or a specified part of it, as part of the pursuer's case.[46] The crucial point here is that the rules require the pursuer to

---

[44] For example, Court of Session PN No 1 of 2017 Paragraph 13a; South Strathclyde Practice Note No 1 of 2022 para 13.

[45] Ibid.

[46] Ibid.

summarise the circumstances out of which the action arises and set out the grounds on which the action proceeds.[47] The key word in the first of those requirements is 'summarise'. That does not require full chapter and verse, but a summary. You do need to append to the summons in a commercial action a schedule listing the documents founded on or adopted as incorporated in the summons, which should also be lodged as an inventory of productions.[48] These documents will commonly contain highly relevant details much of which will not need to be repeated in the pleadings.

That is all well and good but how should you actually go about drafting the condescendence, assuming that some averment of fact is necessary? A useful exercise, maybe using the letter before action as a starting point, is to attempt to summarise your case in plain English on one page of A4 before beginning to draft. This should force you to concentrate on the key issues, and what you must prove in order to succeed.

Try to tell a story in as concise and logical a fashion as possible. Another useful tip is to imagine how the judge's opinion might read at the end of the day, anticipating that it will narrate only those essential facts which have been proved. Those are the facts which you will need to make averments about. Take the common scenario where your landlord client is pursuing a dilapidations claim at the expiry of the lease. You will have to aver that there was a lease and that it has expired; the provisions of that lease which imposed obligations on the tenant; the manner in which the tenant failed to comply with those provisions; and the loss sustained by your client as a result. That is all. If the landlord's interest in the lease has been assigned several times before landing with your client, ask yourself whether that is something that has to be averred if it is not in dispute. If the opinion at the end of the day is unlikely to make reference to that, then there is no need to include detailed averments in your pleadings. As for the breaches of the lease, they

---

[47] RCS r 47.3(2)(c).
[48] RCS r 47.3(3).

will almost certainly be recorded in a schedule which can be referred to and incorporated. Also, avoid the over-use of definitions and capital letters.

Let us try to put that into practice. Consider the following example taken from the introductory article of condescendence in a dilapidations case, where the only issue in dispute between the parties is the extent of the defender's repairing obligations under a lease which has expired:

> The Pursuer is the heritable proprietor of Pentland House, 5 Braids Rigg, Edinburgh, EH97 5XY ('**the Premises**'). It was the landlord, and the Defenders were the tenant, under the Lease of the Premises (as subsequently varied and amended) between The Wise Assurance Company Limited and The Secretary of State for the Environment dated 10 May and 19 June 1990 and registered in the Books of Council and Session on 31 July 1990 ('**the Lease**'). A copy of the Lease is produced. By Minute of Extension of Lease between the Pursuer's then predecessor in title, North Uist Business Parks GP Limited (as trustee for North Uist Business Parks Partnership) and the Defenders, dated 17 and 27 January 2014 and registered in the Books of Council and Session on 21 January 2014, the contractual date of expiry of the Lease was extended until 30 October 2014. By Minute of Extension of Lease between the Pursuer's then predecessor in title, Edinburgh Shopping Centre Limited and the Defenders, dated 26 May and 5 June 2017 and registered in the Books of Council and Session on 3 November 2017, the contractual date of expiry of the Lease was further extended until 30 October 2022 ('**the date of expiry**').

That is not bad but might it be improved? How about this:

> The pursuer is the heritable proprietor of Pentland House, 5 Braids Rigg, Edinburgh. It was the landlord, and the defender the tenant, of that property in terms of a lease (as subsequently varied and amended) between The Wise Assurance Company Limited and The Secretary of State for the Environment dated 10 May and 19 June 1990. A copy of the lease is produced. Following several variations, the contractual date of expiry of the lease was extended until 30 October 2022.

Provided that the date of expiry is not in dispute – which you will know, from the pre-action correspondence – is anything more than that required to introduce the case? Immediately the reader knows that there was a lease of Pentland House between the parties which has expired, and his or her attention is not distracted by unnecessary detail about minutes of extension and, for that matter, unnecessary definitions. The lease is adequately identified by referring to the parties and the dates of execution: that it was registered in the Books of Council and Session is neither here nor there, so that detail need not be averred. There is only one property – Pentland House. There is no need to define it, as 'the premises' or otherwise. For that matter, there is probably no need for its postcode. Likewise, there is only one date of expiry: you can assume that the reader is capable of understanding basic English.

Above all, however you go about it, set out the summons in as concise terms as possible.

Finally, the practical, presentational points bear repeating: try to produce a writ that is easily read. Appearance is important. Avoid single spacing but use 1.5 or double spacing, preferably font size 12. Also, avoid interminable lengthy paragraphs. As a matter of style, it is good practice to split articles of condescendence into sub-articles – e.g. 5.1, 5.2, 5.3 and so on – which makes pleadings much easier to follow. In a similar vein, and going back to the re-worked example above, Do Not Overuse Capitalisation of Terms such as pursuer and defender, which (in the writers' view at least) makes Text less easy on the Eye and more difficult to read.

Once you have drafted the meat of your summons, do not forget to elect to adopt the commercial procedure, which you do by inserting the words 'Commercial Action' immediately below the words 'IN THE COURT OF SESSION'[49] where they occur above the instance (or, in the sheriff court, by using form G1A, which is to similar effect).[50]

---

[49] RCS r 47.3.
[50] OCR r 40.4.

Defences

When it comes to drafting defences in a commercial action, the same general advice applies. The traditional form of pleading need not be followed. In particular – and again this is not always observed – it is not necessary that each averment in the summons should be admitted, not known or denied provided that the extent of the dispute is reasonably well identified. The over-riding requirement, as with the summons, is that fair notice should be given.

The question might be asked, what form should defences take where the only dispute is as to what construction should be placed on a contract or other document, and the above advice is followed, so that the summons consists only of a conclusion, with no condescendence? It is suggested that all that would be required (assuming the defender agrees that the dispute is limited to how the document in question should be construed, and that no factual matrix needs to be averred) would be a brief statement of the contrary interpretation which the defender contended for.

Adjustment

As is common practice in other types of action, adjustments should always be marked on to the summons, defences or other document, indicating the new material using track-changes or strike through, with any changes in a different coloured font. The adjusted document should identify the date of the adjustment.

Four general comments

We would make four other general points about pleading in a commercial action. First, as with all pleading, the first thing you should do is to think. What are the issues? What facts do I need to prove? What facts are in dispute? What facts are not relevant? How can I best summarise the facts? Second, in the paradigm commercial action where the pre-action protocol has been complied with, the summons and defences should really be the finished article and should not need to undergo adjustment in order to properly represent what each party's case is.

Third, the extent to which detailed pleadings are required is ultimately a matter for the commercial judge or sheriff. It is in general easier to add to short pleadings, to give more detail on a particular point, if that is thought to be required, than it is to pare down pleadings which are unnecessarily lengthy.

Finally, as the Practice Notes all emphasise, however concise or brief the pleadings are, there is still very much a requirement for fair notice. As we hope we have made clear this need not always be provided in the pleadings if it can be found elsewhere, but fair notice must still be given. When an allegation of fraud is made, the same standard of relevancy and specification is required as for other pleadings.

Drawing all of the above together, we offer the following list of 'do's and don'ts' for commercial pleadings. Many of these points have been made already but we consider that they are worth repeating. They are worth repeating.

1. *Don't* make excessive use of definitions. The more a piece of writing is cluttered with definitions (as so many modern contracts are), the more difficult it can be to follow. This applies as much to pleadings as to any other writing. If you have already referred once to the Law Reform (Miscellaneous Provisions) Scotland Act 1985, there really is no need to define it as 'the 1985 Act'. It will anyway be obvious what you mean by referring to the 1985 Act. So, too, when you refer to an individual by name. The first time you refer to Jemima Puddleduck there is no need to add in brackets ('Ms Puddleduck') for the reader to understand who Ms Puddleduck is. For the same reason, avoid referring to the 'said' Puddleduck.

2. While on the subject of names, *do* use names rather than initials, which seems to be a modern trend which is creeping in. If the key players are Jemima Puddleduck, Peter Rabbit and Squirrel Nutkin, it is much easier to follow the narrative if they are referred to by those names, rather than the somewhat anodyne JP, PR and SN, often requiring the reader to perform a prodigious feat of memory to work out who is being referred to.

3. *Don't* quote excessively from documents. A concise summary will usually suffice. The document, if material, will be listed in the schedule annexed to the summons (and lodged as a production) and can be read for itself. If it's not material there should be no need to refer to it in the first place. That said, it is permissible to quote directly from a contractual term if crucial to your case, for example the salient parts of a warranty said to have been breached.

4. *Do* break your articles of condescendence down into shorter paragraphs – 5.1, 5.2 and so on. This will encourage the defender to do likewise when responding and will make the pleadings as a whole much easier to read.

5. *Do* use headings. Ditto.

6. *Don't* over-use acronyms. It a term has a recognised acronym – such as the WHO or, possibly, SHA (for shareholder agreement) – then by all means, use it. Or use an acronym if it will allow you to use one short word instead of four or five – particularly if repeated references are required, it is better to refer to SWAN than Scottish Wide Area Network (if you're only going to refer to it once, there is no point). But the CUA (contrived use of acronyms) can simply make pleadings more difficult to follow if the reader constantly has to refer back to the definition, to work out what is being referred to; the more so the more acronyms there are. You don't want your pleadings to end up looking like a script from LOD (*Line of Duty*).

7. *Don't* use old-fashioned, cumbersome and stock expressions such as 'as hereinbefore averred'. Documents are often referred to for their terms and 'incorporated herein for the sake of brevity'. That is at least better (although, ironically, longer) than the Latin phrase it replaces – *brevitatis causa* – but ask yourself, what do the words 'for the sake of brevity' add, other than five unnecessary words? Answer: nothing. Omit them.

8. For that matter, try to avoid the over-use of Latin (except for phrases which are in everyday use in English, such as *prima facie* and *vice versa*. We include in this category the phrases '*quoad ultra*' and '*esto*', which are so ingrained in drafting as to be part of every day (legal) English).

9. *Don't* use two or more words where one will do, or one long word, where a shorter one is better. Rather than 'prior to', why not 'before'? Or say 'later' instead of 'subsequently'. While in commercial actions people tend not to proceed to a *locus*, if they do, then have them going to a place instead.

10. *Do* omit unnecessary details. Enough said.

11. *Do* avoid repetition. Rely on the reader to remember what has already been said. If you have already averred (say) that a wind turbine was installed in November 2018, there is no need to begin a later article of condescendence with 'As hereinbefore condescended upon, the turbine was installed in November 2018'. If you think the reader does require to be reminded of that fact, then, 'As already averred' would be better.

12. *Do* make use of Scott Schedules where appropriate. Where the parties have competing positions on a number of different issues (often in the context of dilapidations claims, but sometimes in other scenarios) it can be very much easier for the reader to see what those respective positions are by looking at a spreadsheet, than by referring to a summons on the one hand, and defences on the other.

Drafting statements of issues

After the lodging of defences, parties have to lodge a statement of issues. While it is open to each party to lodge its own statement, a joint statement, that is, one which has been agreed with your opponent, is heavily encouraged by the court.

The importance of this should not be underestimated. It is your (and your opponent's) opportunity to focus the questions which the commercial judge will eventually have to answer. If you have drafted your summons/defences carefully and properly (and if the pre-action protocol has been observed) it should of course already be obvious what the issues are. Equally, this should be a two-way street, in that the manner in which the statement of issues is drafted should inform what has to go into your pleadings and what can safely be omitted.

How many issues to include? Sometimes there is a fine line between stating issues at too high, and at too low, a level. Don't have a whole series of micro issues. Again, it is suggested that you should try to visualise how the judge's opinion will read. In most cases there are unlikely to be more than five or six issues. Drawing on an example from a personal injuries action, you are unlikely to see an opinion which begins 'There are 29 issues to resolve in this action'. If your first attempt at a statement of issues has 29, then cull it – drastically.

Family actions

Family actions form a significant and important part of court business. They should progress through the court process expeditiously and with as little court procedure as is necessary. To achieve that end, it is the responsibility of the pleader to ensure that from the very outset of the case, the initial writ and defences are prepared with clarity, precision and brevity. While that is doubtless the intention of the majority of practitioners working in this field, in too many cases the 'kitchen sink' approach is adopted. The initial writ is long, pleads evidence and includes irrelevant details not focussed to support the craves. These averments are answered in the defences. They are 'vigorously denied'. They are 'explained and averred' and 'further explained and averred' with more irrelevant detail. Then comes the adjustment. More is added, little removed. Before you know it, the kitchen sink is full to the brim with a record 50 pages long, affidavits running to hundreds of pages, the particular issues for determination at the proof you have next week impossible to identify and your preparation for and prospects at proof … problematic.

That is a nightmare scenario for the solicitors/counsel conducting the case, bamboozling for the clients and a headache for the sheriff/judge hearing your case. Thankfully, it is a situation easily avoided. Written pleadings properly focussed on relevant averments of fact, together with compliance with the relevant rules and practice notes, should combine to avoid unnecessary pitfalls.

What is a family action?

Family actions[51] in the Court of Session are governed by chapter 49 of the Rules of the Court of Session (RCS).[52] In the sheriff court, they are governed by chapter 33 of the Ordinary Cause Rules (OCR).

A 'family action' is any action falling within the definition provided by rule 49.1 of the RCS and rule 33.1 of the OCR. They include actions of divorce, separation, declarators of marriage, legitimacy/illegitimacy, parentage/non-parentage, legitimation, financial provision, orders under section 11 of the Children (Scotland) Act 1995 ('section 11 orders'), aliment, etc. If your case falls within the definition of those rules, your action requires to be raised according to those rules.

Drafting in family cases – the basics

In the Court of Session, the pleadings are set out in a summons in form 13.2-A and answers in accordance with rules 18.1 to 18.3. In addition, specific averments are required depending on the nature of the actions. These are set out in chapter 49 and are largely the same as required in the sheriff court.

In the sheriff court, the pleadings are contained in an initial writ and defences.[53] The general principles for drafting an initial writ and defences per Chapters 2 and 3 above should be adhered to. However, there are some particular points of drafting that must be complied with in family cases (see further below).

Since the vast majority of family actions are raised in the sheriff court, this chapter focuses on pleadings in the sheriff court.

---

[51] Save for adoptions, in respect of which there are bespoke rules. See further below.

[52] The Court of Session has concurrent jurisdiction with the sheriff court in relation to the vast majority of family cases; see further, Macphail, *Sheriff Court Practice*, ch 2, para 2.74.

[53] Initial writ in form G1 per OCR r 3.1.1(a) and defences conform to OCR r 33.36F.

Divorce – are pleadings required?

Before turning to the drafting of family pleadings, bear in mind that if your client is seeking decree of divorce, an initial writ might not be necessary. If the conditions set out in rule 33.73(1) are satisfied, your client can apply for divorce in terms of the 'simplified divorce' procedure utilising a form rather than pleadings (hurrah!).[54]

Family pleadings generally

Precognition

The importance of taking a detailed precognition before drafting any family pleadings cannot be overstated.[55] You will do your client no favours by hastily cobbling together a writ spawned of a thousand emails and a zillion attachments.

Where, who and what?

A bewildering array of matters are required, by the court rules, to be included in your family pleadings depending on the circumstances. The first is *where* you should be raising the action and why. Related to that, is *who* needs (formally per the rules) to know about the action. Lastly, you may be obliged to aver *what* the facts are on specific matters.

You **must** therefore familiarise yourself with the rules applicable to your action before commencing any drafting. If you do not, you are bound to omit something important inevitably leading to (i) the bouncing of your writ by the court; (ii) a dreaded call to your client to explain why you need yet more information from them when you said the action would be raised yesterday.

---

[54] See OCR r 33.73 to 33.82; application in forms F31, F33 or F33A (depending on the ground of divorce) lodged with the necessary documents and fee.

[55] All the more important following the introduction of new case management rules in the sheriff court (see further below). See also Chapter 2 on precognitions.

The following is a summary of specific matters required by the rules to be averred in your pleadings.

Where?

If you are acting for the pursuer you need to aver in the first article of condescendence why the court has jurisdiction. The following is a summary only on jurisdiction in the most common family cases.[56]

Jurisdiction: Section 11 orders

If your case relates to a 'section 11 order',[57] jurisdiction is governed by the Family Law Act 1986, sections 8 to 15. In essence, in sheriff court cases, the action should be raised in the sheriffdom in which the child is habitually resident.[58] In Court of Session actions the requirement is that the child is habitually resident in Scotland.[59] An averment should be included to that effect in the first article of condescendence. It is sometimes necessary to make an emergency application to the court for orders relating to a child in situations where the child is not habitually resident within the sheriffdom/Scotland. While those situations are rare, careful consideration to jurisdiction, with reference to the 1986 Act, should be given, in order that appropriate averments relating to jurisdiction can be made.

Jurisdiction: divorce, separation, etc.

In relation to actions for divorce, separation, declarator of nullity of marriage and declarator of marriage, jurisdiction is governed by the Domicile and Matrimonial Proceedings Act 1973.[60] In general, the sheriff court has jurisdiction if (i) either party to the marriage is domiciled in Scotland on the

---

[56] For a more detailed appraisal, see Macphail, *Sheriff Court Practice*, paras 2.74 to 2.85, and para 22.03; and E M Clive, *The Law of Husband and Wife in Scotland*, 4th edn (1997).

[57] Children (Scotland) Act 1995, s 11.

[58] Family Law Act 1986, s 9(b).

[59] Family Law Act 1986, s 9(a).

[60] Sections 7 (Court of Session) and 8 (sheriff court).

date when the action is begun or was habitually resident there throughout the period of one year ending with that date *and* (ii) either party to the marriage was resident in the sheriffdom for a period of 40 days ending with the date on which the action began or had been resident in the sheriffdom for a period of not less than 40 days ending not more than 40 days before the date on which the action commenced and has no known residence in Scotland at that date.[61] The Court of Session has jurisdiction if either of the parties is domiciled in Scotland on the date when the action is begun or was habitually resident in Scotland throughout the period of one year ending with that date.[62] You must include averments to this effect in the first article of condescendence.

Jurisdiction: dissolution of civil partnership, etc.

In relation to actions for dissolution/separation of a civil partnership, the sheriff court has jurisdiction if either party is (i) domiciled in Scotland on the date when proceedings are begun or (ii) either party was habitually resident in Scotland throughout the period of one year ending with that date; and (iii) either civil partner was resident in the sheriffdom for a period of 40 days ending with the date when the action is begun or (iv) had been resident in the sheriffdom for a period of not less than 40 days ending not more than 40 days before that date and has no known residence in Scotland at that date.[63] Only parts (i) and (ii) above have to be satisfied for the Court of Session to have jurisdiction. If neither applies, it may still have jurisdiction if the parties registered as civil partners of each other in Scotland, and no court has or is recognised as having jurisdiction and it appears to the court to be in the interests of justice to assume jurisdiction in the case.[64] Whatever the ground is, you're averring it in article one of condescendence.

---

[61] Domicile and Matrimonial Proceedings Act 1973, s 8(2).

[62] Domicile and Matrimonial Proceedings Act 1973, s 7(2A).

[63] Civil Partnership Act 2004, s 225.

[64] Civil Partnership Act 2004 s 225(1)(c).

The 'who': warrants for intimation

On whom does the writ require to be intimated? As well as the parties to the action, rule 33(7) OCR provides that warrants for intimation on particular persons must be craved in certain circumstances, or alternatively a crave to dispense with intimation on that particular person in certain other circumstances. A full appraisal of the various circumstances in which intimation is required to be made to particular persons is helpfully set out in Macphail.[65] Style craves for warrants to intimate can be found in *Green's Litigation Styles*.

The following summarises the most common scenarios. In all such cases, you should include a crave for warrant to intimate on the particular person together with supporting factual averments in the condescendence:

Defender's whereabouts unknown/defender has a mental disorder
It sometimes happens that the pursuer to an action for divorce does not know the address of the defender. Reasonable efforts should be made to trace their whereabouts via sheriff officers/tracing agents. If that proves unsuccessful and the address cannot be reasonably ascertained, a warrant for intimation on every child of the marriage who has reached the age of 16 and to one of defender's next of kin (aged over 16) should be craved, if the address of those persons can reasonably be ascertained.[66] In the case of any person whose address cannot reasonably be ascertained, the pursuer should crave for intimation on that person to be dispensed with. You must aver that the address of the defender is not known, and the steps taken to ascertain the address.[67]

A crave for warrant to intimate upon the same class of persons (child over 16 and defender's next of kin) should be included where the defender is suffering from a mental disorder

---

[65] Macphail, *Sheriff Court Practice*, ch 22, para 22.09.
[66] OCR r 33.7(1)(a)(i) and (ii); intimation upon such persons is made using form F1; and see also Macphail, *Sheriff Court Rules*, ch 22, para 22.09.
[67] OCR r 33.4.

within the meaning of section 328 of the Mental Health (Care and Treatment) (Scotland) Act 2003.[68] A warrant for intimation upon any guardian appointed for the defender should also be included.[69]

Section 11 orders in respect of a child of the marriage/one of the parties to the action

In all cases in which the pursuer seeks a section 11 order in relation to a child who is *not* a party to the action, you must either crave warrant to intimate on the child to seek their views or include a crave seeking dispensation of intimation on the child (for example that the child would be too young to provide a view).[70] Where the action is to be intimated on the child, you do so by way of a Form F9 only, in which the child is invited to provide views on the particular points contained within the form. A draft F9 should be lodged with the writ at warranting stage. The F9 is an important part of the overall drafting process. As Macphail notes:

> The style form appended to the rules provides a framework, however, the pursuer must submit a bespoke, draft Form F9 when presenting the initial writ for warranting. The draft should take into consideration the age of the child and reflect the craves of the action, the orders sought or the issues upon which the child may wish to express a view.[71]

Where a pursuer seeks a section 11 order, you must crave for a warrant to intimate upon any parent or guardian of the child who is *not* a party to the action.[72]

In any action for divorce, separation, declarator of marriage or declarator of nullity of marriage, where the sheriff may make a section 11 order in respect of a child who is:

[68] OCR r 33.7(1)(c)(i).
[69] OCR r 33.7(1)(c)(ii).
[70] OCR r 33.7A.
[71] Macphail, *Sheriff Court Practice*, ch 22, para 22.17.
[72] OCR r 33.7(1)(f).

- In the care of the local authority, a warrant for intimation upon the local authority should be sought.[73]

- The child of only one party to the marriage but has been accepted as a child of the family by the other party to the marriage, and is liable to be maintained by a *third party*, intimation should be made to the third party. Intimation should also be made to any third party who exercises care and control of the child.[74]

Divorce on the ground of adultery

In a divorce action where the pursuer alleges that the defender has committed adultery with another person, the pursuer should (subject to certain exceptions) crave warrant for intimation on that person.[75]

Financial provision cases

If the pursuer is seeking an order for transfer of property under section 8(1)(aa) of the Family Law (Scotland) Act 1985 and the consent of a third party is necessary by virtue of any obligation, enactment or rule of law or the property is subject to a security, intimation should be made upon the third party/creditor.[76]

If seeking an order under section 18 of the Family Law (Scotland) Act 1985 relating to avoidance transactions, you must intimate upon any third party in whose favour the transfer of, or transaction involving the property was or is to be made and any other person having an interest in such a transfer or transaction.[77]

In applications by a non-entitled partner under the Matrimonial Homes (Family Protection) (Scotland) Act 1981, intimation may be needed on any spouse of the entitled partner, or in certain applications, intimation may be required on a

---

[73] OCR r 33.7(1)(e)(i) with intimation in form 5.
[74] OCR r 33.7(e)(ii) and (iii) with intimation in form 6.
[75] OCR r 33.7(b) with any intimation in form 2.
[76] OCR r 33.7(i) with intimation in form 10.
[77] OCR r 33.7(j) with intimation in form 11.

third party (e.g. a landlord) if the entitled partner/spouse occupies the home as a tenant.[78]

In applications for financial provision relating to a party's pension (e.g. a pension sharing order), intimation should be made on the trustees/managers of the pension scheme to which the application relates.[79]

Application under section 29(2) of the Family Law (Scotland) Act 2006

A pursuer making an application under section 29(2) of the Family Law (Scotland) Act 2006 must include the deceased's executor as a defender to the action.[80] In addition, a crave for warrant to intimate on any person having an interest in the deceased's net estate should be included.[81]

Persons upon whom intimation required but identity/whereabouts unknown

In all cases where the identity or address of a person to whom intimation is required is not known and cannot reasonably be ascertained, you crave to dispense with intimation on that basis and include averments to that effect.[82]

The 'what': averments required by the rules
Other proceedings already commenced

In actions of divorce, separation, declarator of marriage or declarator of nullity of marriage, you need to aver whether, to the knowledge of the pursuer, any proceedings are continuing in Scotland or in any other country in respect of the marriage to which the initial writ relates, or are capable of affecting its validity or subsistence.[83] In the vast majority of cases there will be no such proceedings and the averment will simply confirm

---

[78] OCR r 33.7(k) with intimation in form 12.
[79] OCR r 33.7(l) to (o) with intimation in forms F12A to D.
[80] OCR r 33.6A(1).
[81] OCR r 33.7(p) with intimation in form F12E.
[82] OCR r 33.7(5).
[83] OCR r 33.2(2)(a).

that. However, that should not be assumed. It is an important question to ask your client at the first meeting. If there are other proceedings raised elsewhere, you must specify in the averments the name of the court, tribunal or authority before which the proceedings have been commenced; the date of commencement; name of the parties; the date of any proof in the proceedings; and any such other facts as are relevant to the question of whether the proceedings to which the initial writ relates should be sisted.[84]

Similarly, in actions for divorce, separation or declarator of nullity of marriage in which a section 11 order is sought, there must be an averment confirming whether or not there are any proceedings already commenced in relation to the child in respect of whom the section 11 order is sought.[85] In any other family actions, the same averment should be included *and* there should be averments as to whether there are any proceedings already commenced relating to the *marriage* of the parents of the child.[86]

In actions in which a section 11 order is craved, there should be an averment confirming that no permanence order is in force in relation to the child.[87]

In the event that the individual applying for the section 11 order omits these details, it is the responsibility of the opposing party to include the particulars of any such other proceedings.[88]

Maintenance orders

In a family action in which an order for aliment or periodical allowance is sought (including a variation or recall) by any party, you must aver whether and, if so, when and by whom a maintenance order (within the meaning of section 106 of the Debtors (Scotland) Act 1987) has been granted in favour of or

---

[84] OCR r 33.2(2)(b)(i) to (v).
[85] OCR r 33.3(1)(a).
[86] OCR r 33.3(1)(b).
[87] OCR r 33.3(1)(c).
[88] OCR r 33.3(2).

against that party of any other person in respect of whom the order is sought.[89]

Aliment

Certain averments are mandatory if your client is craving aliment. What is required depends upon whether section 8(6), (7), (8) or (10) of the Child Support Act 1991 Act applies or not. If they do, the averments contained at rule 33.6(2) should be included. In addition, the writ should be accompanied by any document issued by the Secretary of State to the party intimating the making of the maintenance calculation.[90]

Where the above sections under the 1991 Act do *not* apply and a crave for aliment is sought, the averments required per rule 33.6(3) should be included.[91]

In an action for declarator of non-parentage or illegitimacy, the initial writ requires to contain averments as to whether the pursuer previously was alleged to be the parent in an application for a maintenance calculation under sections 4, 5 or 7 of the 1991 Act. Where an allegation of paternity has been made against the pursuer, the Secretary of State requires to be named as a defender in the action.[92]

A family action involving parties in respect of whom a decision has been made in any application, review or appeal under the 1991 Act relating to any child of the parties shall include averments stating that such a decision has been made and give the details of that decision. Unless the sheriff on cause shown otherwise directs, the writ shall also be accompanied by any document issued by the Secretary of State to the parties intimating that decision.[93]

Divorce on the ground of issue of an interim gender recognition certificate

If your action relates to divorce on the ground of an interim gender recognition certificate having been issued to either

---

[89] OCR r 33.5.
[90] OCR r 33.6(2).
[91] OCR r 33.6(3).
[92] OCR r 33.6(4).
[93] OCR r 33.6(5).

party, certain averments require to be included by the pursuer.[94] If it was the pursuer to whom the certificate was issued, the pursuer should aver whether the Gender Recognition Panel has issued a full gender recognition certificate to the pursuer.[95] Where the defender is the party to whom the certificate was issued, the pursuer should aver whether since the issue of the certificate the pursuer has made a statutory declaration consenting to the marriage continuing and whether the panel has given the pursuer notice of the issue of the full gender recognition certificate to the defender.[96]

What next?

After nailing down the obligatory craves/averments, the general guidance in Chapter 2 on drafting an initial writ should be followed. The particular orders sought by your client in a family action (particularly in an action for financial provision on divorce) may be numerous. *Green's Litigation Styles* contains an example of almost every type of crave that will be necessary in family cases.[97]

In the first article of condescendence the basis of jurisdiction should be set out, as well as confirmation as to whether any other proceedings are continuing in Scotland or elsewhere.

In the second article of condescendence in actions relating to a marriage or civil partnership, you need to aver that the parties are married/in a civil partnership and the date and place of marriage/civil partnership. An extract marriage/civil partnership certificate should be lodged with the writ. Similarly, the names and dates of birth of the children of the parties to the marriage/civil partnership (or who have been assumed as such a child) should be averred in full, and extract birth certificates lodged with the writ. In an action for section 11 orders, you should include averments here if seeking to dispense with intimation of an F9, for example 'Jane Bloggs is

---

[94] OCR r 33.6ZA.
[95] OCR r 33.6ZA(2)(a).
[96] OCR r 33.6ZA(2)(b).
[97] See also Chapter 2 above.

two years of age and would not be capable of understanding the present proceedings. She is not yet able to read or write. It would accordingly be inappropriate to give intimation to her of the present proceedings or to seek her views through the use of a form F9'.

In cases relating to divorce/dissolution of civil partnership, the next step is usually to aver what happened next. Remember, brevity is key. Unless relevant to the ground on which divorce is craved (e.g. unreasonable behaviour or adultery) it is rarely relevant to include an averment beyond setting out that after the marriage/civil partnership the parties lived together until a particular date, namely, the date on which the parties separated. That date determines the point in time from which the clock starts running in relation to divorces based on non-cohabitation[98] (the majority of divorces) but is also the date after which any property acquired by the parties ceases to be matrimonial property (the 'relevant date').[99] It is an important line in the sand. While parties are often clear on the date on which they separated, that is not always the case. Sometimes, this will be a disputed issue (for example, if there have been reconciliation attempts and/or the date has a significant bearing on financial provision). It should be an important focus of your first meeting with your client/their precognition.

If that date can be specified precisely, it is necessary to set out that the parties have not lived together since that date; that the marriage has broken down irretrievably and there is no prospect of reconciliation between the parties. If the defender consents to divorce, the signed form of consent should be produced. So, for example, in the third article of condescendence in a divorce action based on two years non-cohabitation it might read something like this: 'After the marriage the parties lived together until around 10 August 2022. They then separated and have not lived together as husband and wife since. The marriage has broken down irretrievably. There is

---

[98] Divorce (Scotland) Act 1976, s 1(c) and (d).
[99] Family Law (Scotland) Act 1985, s 10.

no prospect of a reconciliation between the parties. The pursuer now seeks decree of divorce'.

In an action for a section 11 order, for example, a residence order, the third article of condescendence will set out that the parties separated on a particular date and then explain the children's particular circumstances and why the order is necessary. Depending on the extent of the information, that might be set out over a number of articles of condescendence. As a basic example:

> Since the parties' separation the children have resided with the purser at 1 Law Avenue, Edinburgh. There is ample accommodation for the children and the pursuer in the property, which is a three bedroom detached house with front and rear garden. Joe Bloggs attends the local primary school and Jane Bloggs attends the local nursery, both of which are within walking distance from the property. They are happy and well cared for by the pursuer. The pursuer is not employed and is available to care for them at all times. Joe Bloggs has expressed a desire to continue living with the pursuer. Both children have had regular contact with the defender. On several occasions since 1 October 2023, the defender has repeatedly told Joe Bloggs that he is making arrangements for the children to reside with him. On each of these occasions Joe Bloggs has returned from contact upset and distressed at the prospect of having to live with the defender. His sleep is disturbed. He is upset and anxious at school. The children require stability and security. It is accordingly in their best interests that the order be made. It would be better for them that it be made than no order be made.

Pleas-in-law

Pleas-in-law are required in family actions as they are in ordinary actions. In relation to the examples given above, the plea-in-law for the divorce would be, 'the marriage of the parties having irretrievably broken down by reason of non-cohabitation for over two years, decree of divorce should be granted as craved'. For the residence order, 'it being in the best interests of the children that a residence order providing that they live with the pursuer should be made and it being better for them that such an order be made than not be made, decree should be pronounced as craved'.

The examples given are purposefully simplistic. Every writ should be drafted according to the particular circumstances of the case.

Defences

The standard procedure in ordinary defended actions (chapters 9 and 10 of the OCR) does not apply to family actions. If defending a family action you must lodge with the court and intimate to the pursuer a notice of intention to defend in form F26.[100] Defences must be lodged within 14 days after the expiry of the period of notice and be in the form of answers in numbered paragraphs corresponding to the articles of condescendence and contain pleas-in-law of the defender.[101]

Where the defender in a family action seeks an order in the proceedings, for example aliment, an order for financial provision,[102] a section 11 order or an order for financial provision under section 28 or 29 of the Family Law (Scotland) Act 2006, you must include craves for same in the defences, averments in the answers to the condescendence in support of those craves and appropriate pleas-in-law.[103] Where the defender opposes the pursuer's crave for financial provision and/or makes their own claim for financial provision the defender must lodge with the defences a signed Form F13A.[104]

Similarly, any defender seeking a section 11 order in respect of a child who is not a party to the action is subject to the same requirements regarding a crave for intimation/to dispense with intimation, draft form F9 and averments as apply to pursuers.

So, for example, in an action in which the pursuer seeks a section 11 residence order, and the defender wants a section 11

---

[100] OCR r 33.34(2)(a).

[101] OCR r 33.36F; see also the requirements of any counterclaim.

[102] Within the meaning of section 8(3) of the Family Law (Scotland) Act 1985 (see OCR r 33.34(1)(b)(ii)).

[103] OCR r 33.34(2)(b)).

[104] OCR r 33.34(4).

contact order made in their favour, the defences will include a crave (after the instance) as follows:

The defender craves the court to:
1. make a contact order providing for Joe Bloggs to have direct contact with the defender on alternate weekends from 10am on a Saturday until 7pm on a Sunday, or during such times and periods as shall seem appropriate to the court.
2. for warrant to intimate these proceedings to Joe Bloggs;
3. for the expenses of the action against the pursuer.

The answers should, as well as answering the averments in the initial writ, contain averments supporting the crave sought in the defences. The averments in the initial writ should be answered first according to the general principles set out in Chapter 2. After the all-important '*quoad ultra* denied' you should state 'explained and averred' and then provide the averments setting out why the order craved is necessary/should be granted.

As well as the pleas-in-law answering the case against you, a plea-in-law supportive of the craves you seek also requires to be included. So, in the section 11 order case example:

It not being better for the child that a residence order be made than not be made, decree as craved by the pursuer should be refused.

It being in the best interests of the child for a contact order to be made, and it being better for the child than the order be made than not be made, decree should be granted as craved by the defender.

Pitfalls in adjustment
Reference is made to Chapter 4 above in relation to adjustment of pleadings. The same principles apply to family actions.

As with the drafting of the initial writ and defences, only averments relevant to support the crave/give notice to the other side as to your case should be included at adjustment stage. Despite that, perhaps because of the importance of the proceedings to the parties and any children in respect of whom orders are sought, in very many cases the pleadings are endlessly long, and made longer at adjustment stage. It is not uncommon to see, added at adjustment stage, reference to what was said by parties' agents (and worse still, the sheriff (!)) at an earlier Child Welfare Hearing. Quite apart from any such averments not being relevant to the ground of action, think about what happens at the proof if those averments are included. Do you intend to give evidence at the proof to prove these averments? Will you be citing your opponent? Do you intend to cite the sheriff to do the same? What happened at an earlier child welfare hearing, or any earlier procedural hearing, should be left out of the writ/defences. If your opponent has made the mistake of including any such irrelevant averment, do not be drawn into responding substantively to them. Something along the lines of 'Admitted that a child welfare hearing took place on 1 February 2023 beyond which no admission is made' followed by the all-important '*quoad ultra* denied' would suffice.

Case management in family cases
Actions commenced on or after 25 September 2023 are now subject to new case management rules, designed to progress defended family actions expeditiously and to allow consistent and effective judicial case management.[105] It is important that you read the rules before drafting your pleadings. Why? Because, within 49 days of the last date for lodging the notice of intention to defend, you will be appearing at an Interim Case Management Hearing before a sheriff expecting you to address them on all the matters required by the rules – all matters more commonly seen at a pre-proof hearing.[106] A further Full Case Management Hearing will see you do the same,[107] only this time you are on a high-speed train, beyond the point of adjustment, and the next stop is the proof. There's no point

---

[105] Act of Sederunt (Ordinary Cause Rules 1993 Amendment) (Case Management of Defended Family and Civil Partnership Acts) 2022/289 SSI, para 3; see OCR r 33.36A onwards.
[106] OCR r 33.36J(3)(a) to (p).
[107] OCR r 33.36P(3)(a) to (p).

asking for endless continuations either. The rules don't allow them.

So, at the point in time you are drafting your pleadings they should be near enough 'proof ready'. To do that you need to know and understand your case from as early a point as possible.

Amendment

The general principles relating to amendment set out in Chapter 4 apply equally to family actions.

Undefended actions

When no notice of intention to defend has been lodged, your drafting is not necessarily at an end. Unless the action falls under one of the listed exceptions in rule 33.28(1) (a) (i) to (vii) affidavit evidence requires to be lodged in accordance with that rule, together with a minute in form F27.[108] The form of the affidavit, how many affidavits are required and from whom and the matters the affidavit should address should conform to the practice notes applicable in the particular sheriffdom/the Court of Session.[109]

Minute and Answer procedure

It often happens in family actions that after final decree is pronounced, a party needs further orders from the court. If the orders sought arise from the same circumstances/relate to the

---

[108] OCR r 33.28.

[109] For Sheriff Court Practice Notes see: https://www.scotcourts.gov.uk/rules-and-practice/practice-notes-and-directions/#/. The applicable Practice Notes as at the time of writing in the sheriff court are: Tayside Central & Fife, No 2 of 2023; Glasgow and Strathkelvin, No 3 of 2018; Grampian Highland and Islands, No 1 of 2003; Lothian and Borders, No 4 of 2018; South Strathclyde Dumfries & Galloway No 1 of 2003; and North Strathclyde, the Consolidated Practice Note 2017. See also the Court of Session practice Note on same, No 1 of 2018.

same parties in the original action the procedure used is one of Minute and Answer, lodged in the original court process.

The court rules provide the circumstances in which the Minute and Answer procedure should be utilised.[110] The most commonly utilised Minute and Answer procedure in family cases relates to applications to vary/recall section 11 orders after final decree.[111]

The general procedure relating to the lodging of such Minutes is contained within Chapter 14 of the rules. In particular, the Minute must contain a crave, a condescendence in the form of a statement of facts supporting the crave, and pleas-in-law.[112] The content of the Minute is therefore much like an initial writ. Similarly, depending on the nature of the application, there may be specific craves/averments you are required to include. For example, in applications relation to a section 11 order, warrant to intimate on the child.[113]

If your Minute follows a decision having been made by the sheriff after proof, and contained within a written judgment, it is unnecessary to make extensive reference in your Minute to the evidence led at proof, or indeed to quote from the court's written judgment. Such averments will rarely be relevant.

---

[110] For example, in an action of divorce, separation or declarator of nullity of marriage, an application after final decree for, or for the variation or recall of a section 11 order or regarding the enforcement of such an order, is made by Minute in the process of the action to which the application relates (OCR r 33.44); the same goes for an application after final decree for, or for the variation or recall of an order for aliment (OCR r 33.45 and 33.46); and for certain applications for financial provision after final decree of divorce (OCR r 33.51).

[111] OCR r 33.44, and see the warrants for intimation and averments required in any such minute at OCR r 33.44A to 33.44D; see also Macphail, *Sheriff Court Practice*, ch 22, para 22.57 to 22.59.

[112] OCR r 14.2. Note that a condescendence and pleas-in-law are only required per the rules 'where appropriate'. In the writers' view, it will always be appropriate where the application is for/a variation/recall of a section 11 order.

[113] OCR r 33.44A.

Remember, it is facts necessary to support the craves that should be averred, not a full procedural history of the action, or your own gloss on the evidence of the parties at proof, or a selection of the best and most memorable quotes from the court's decision. So, by way of an example, in an application for variation of a contact order made in a divorce action, the appropriate averments would be:

> The parties were married on 1 October 2007 and divorced in this court on 10 April 2022. In terms of the said decree of divorce, the minuter was found entitled to contact with the said child Joe Bloggs born 2 December 2018 each alternate Sunday from 9am until 12pm. The minuter seeks a variation of that order. This court has jurisdiction.[114]

Thereafter, the relevant facts to support a variation of the order will relate to what the material change in the parties'/child's circumstances are that justify the original order being varied. That will involve setting out, for example, what has happened since the order was made (for example, that the minuter and the child have enjoyed the fortnightly contact, that the child has expressed a desire to have residential contact with the minuter) and why the order should be granted (for example, that the minuter has suitable accommodation for such contact to take place, why it is in the child's best interests to have the contact craved for in the Minute and why the proceedings are necessary). An appropriate plea-in-law should be inserted after the statement of facts, for example,

> There having been a material change in circumstances, a variation of the said contact arrangements being in the best interests of the child and it being better for him that the order now sought be made than that no further order be made at all, decree should be granted as craved.[115]

---

[114] See *Green's Litigation Styles*, paras I05-27B and I05-27C.
[115] Ibid.

The form and content of the Answers ordered by the court generally follow those of defences to an initial writ, save for the fact that they will be headed up 'Answers to Minute for Variation'.

Adoptions and permanence orders

Applications for adoption and permanence orders in terms of the Adoption and Children (Scotland) Act 2007 are raised either in the sheriff court or the Court of Session.[116] In the sheriff court such applications are governed by the Act of Sederunt (Sheriff Court Rules Amendment) (Adoption and Children (Scotland) Act 2007) 2009 (SSI 2009/284). In the Court of Session, the procedure is set out in chapter 67 of the Rules of the Court of Session. In general, the procedure is designed to be straightforward, to be conducted expeditiously without undue delay and the rules to be interpreted flexibly to reflect that the welfare of the child is the court's paramount consideration.[117]

Traditional written pleadings are dispensed with. The application for adoption/permanence orders is by petition using the particular form prescribed by the rules.[118] A detailed assessment of the law relating to adoptions and permanence orders is beyond the scope of this book. However, the pleader cannot

---

[116] Adoption and Children (Scotland) Act 2007, s 118. If the application relates to a child who is in Scotland when the application is made, the appropriate court is the Court of Session or the sheriff court of the sheriffdom in which the child is. In cases where the application is for an adoption order or a permanence order seeking provision granting authority for the child to whom the order relates to be adopted and the child is *not* in Scotland when the application is made, the appropriate court is the Court of Session.

[117] See Macphail, *Sheriff Court Practice*, ch 29, paras 29.01 and 02; and see generally M Jack, *Adoption of Children in Scotland*, 5th edn (2016).

[118] In the sheriff court, adoption applications are made in form 1 (adoption rule 8); permanence order applications in form 11 (adoption rule 31); in the Court of Session, adoption applications are made in form 67.8A (RCS r 67.8 and permanence order applications in form 67.28 per RCS r ... 67.28!)

go far wrong if the petition is drafted by inserting the information requested on the particular form of petition. Comprising a series of numbered paragraphs the form tells you exactly what information requires to be inserted. They should be read together with the rules and the legislation in order to be drafted correctly.

A separate form of petition should be drafted for each child, even where an adoption/permanence order application is made in respect of two or more children from the same family.

Opposed applications

In the sheriff court, following intimation on the relevant persons required by the rules,[119] any such person who intends to oppose the application must lodge and intimate a form of response[120] not later than the 21 days or, if the sheriff has directed another period, the period provided for in the form of intimation. The form of response, unlike a notice of intention to defend, should contain a brief statement of the reasons for opposition.

The lodging of the form of response triggers further drafting for the petitioner. Within 14 days of the form of response being lodged, the petitioner must lodge a statement in terms of rules 16A (adoptions) and 34A (permanence orders) setting out the facts on which the petitioner intends to rely, including averments in relation to the specific matters listed in rules 16A and 34A. There is a temptation at this stage to simply copy and paste the content of the reporting officer/*curator ad litem*'s report. Don't do it! You should review the content of reports and productions and plead the factual averments that will be relied upon in support of the application and will form the foundation of the evidence to be lead at proof.

The court will order the respondent to lodge answers to the rule 16A/34A statement within a particular timescale. Like

---

[119] See adoption rule 14 (adoption) and adoption rule 33 (permanence orders).

[120] Form 8 in adoptions (adoption rule 16) and form 15 in permanence orders (adoption rule 34).

answers in any petition process or defences in an ordinary action, the respondent should answer every averment of fact and provide notice of any substantive defence to the action. The answers should be in numbered paragraphs corresponding to the rule 16A/34A statement. There is no provision in the rules for the pleadings to be adjusted.

In the Court of Session, any person on whom the petition has been intimated and who wishes to oppose the application requires to attend the hearing on the By Order roll (similar to the preliminary hearing) to be heard, at which the court shall make an order for answers to be lodged by the respondent.

Concluding comments
Family disputes are frequently messy, complicated and challenging. Family *pleadings* needn't be any of those things. Every case is capable of being pled in a straightforward way. Clear. Concise. The solid anchor to which your case is grounded. When feeling adrift you would do well to remember this: 'legal writing should focus on the solution, not how big the problem is. The judge needs to be helped to shore, not drowned in paper'.[121]

Petitions

What is a petition?
The first thing you will need to think about when drafting any Court of Session writ is whether the action should proceed by way of summons or petition. Usually it will be obvious. A dispute which involves one person vindicating their rights against another – for example, an action for payment of a debt, or for damages or interdict – proceeds by way of summons. Equally, it is well established that an application to vary trust purposes, or for liquidation of a company or for reduction of a company's share capital, or to invoke the supervisory jurisdiction of the court, must proceed by way of petition. However, it is not

---

[121] I Morley, *The Devil's Advocate*, 3rd edn (2015) at p 159.

always that straightforward. Sometimes, either a summons or a petition might be competent. If in doubt, it is well worth reading the discussion of the difference between an ordinary Court of Session action and a petition in *Hooley Ltd* v *Ganges Jute Private Ltd*.[122] At its most basic, a petition is an application to the court seeking the aid of the court for some purpose or other,[123] generally in one of two situations: where the court is being asked for good reason to go beyond the existing law; or where it is asked to pronounce an order that may have an effect on third parties.

The form of a petition

Having decided that you need to draft a petition (and assuming you have rights of audience enabling you to do so), the basic rules of drafting which apply to summons also apply to petitions, but things are done in a different order, and there is no need at all for pleas-in-law.[124] However, there are certain formalities which must be observed. Other than petitions for judicial review, discussed below, a petition must be in Form 14.4 of the Court of Session Rules. The instance must set out the name, designation and address of the petitioner only (not that of the respondent(s)) and state any special capacity in which the petitioner is presenting the petition.[125] It is customary also to state the nature of the order sought: for example, an order to rectify a mis-statement in a notice delivered to the Registrar of Companies in terms of section 859M of the Companies Act 2006.

The petition begins with the words 'HUMBLY SHEWETH'[126] and then must set out in numbered paragraphs the facts and circumstances giving rise to the petition[127] (each beginning 'That', although, somewhat ungrammatically, this is

---

[122] [2019] CSIH 40, 2019 SC 632, an example of a case where summons and petition procedure were both competent.

[123] *Tomkins* v *Cohen* 1951 SC 22 at 23 per Lord Keith.

[124] Except in petitions for judicial review, covered later.

[125] RCS r 14.4(2)(c).

[126] The drift towards the use of modern English in other forms of pleading not yet having caught up with petitions.

[127] RCS r 14.4(2)(a).

not always observed), before moving on to the prayer (a crave by any other name, but one which appears at the end of the writ rather than at the beginning), setting out the orders which the petitioner seeks.[128] Ideally, this should be in chronological, or at least a logical, order, and if the subject matter of the petition is complicated, do not be afraid to use headings or sub-paragraphs.

The prayer must also crave warrant for such intimation, service and advertisement as may be necessary having regard to the nature of the petition. It is impossible to give hard and fast rules about what intimation, service and advertisement might be required, since that depends entirely on the nature of the petition. Generally, the court will expect service on or intimation to all persons who might have an interest (and the more such persons there might be, the greater the need for advertisement). You then have to set out the name, address and capacity of each person on whom service is sought in a schedule annexed to the petition, referred to in the prayer.[129] If you wish to dispense with intimation, service or advertisement for any reason, or to shorten (or, less usually, extend) the period of notice, that has to be craved in the prayer, supported by averments in the statement of facts setting out the grounds for doing so. Where statutory provisions are founded upon, it is common practice nowadays to incorporate these in an appendix to the petition: in the above example, section 859I to 859M of the Companies Act 2006.

Petitions for judicial review
When drafting a petition for judicial review, many of the usual rules applicable to pleadings generally, and for that matter, to petitions, fly out the proverbial window. Rule 14.4 is disapplied.[130] Instead, a petition for judicial review must be in Form 58.3.[131] All relevant documents in the petitioner's possession

---

[128] RCS r 14.4(2)(b).
[129] RCS r 14.4(5).
[130] RCS r 58.1(3)(a).
[131] RCS r 58.3(3).

or control must be lodged with the petition,[132] and the petition must also have appended to it a schedule specifying any documents which the petitioner founds upon that are not in the petitioner's possession or control, and the person who does have possession or control of those documents.[133]

Form 58.3 requires the petitioner's designation and address to be stated in the instance, followed by the words 'for judicial review of', followed by a brief description of the matter sought to be reviewed. The Form is then in the following terms:

1. That the petitioner is as designed in the instance. The respondent[s] is [or are] as designed in Part 1 of the Schedule for Service. [The persons specified in Part 2 of the Schedule for Service may have an interest.] The petitioner has standing. (*State the standing of the petitioner.*)

2. That the date on which the grounds giving rise to the petition first arose was (*date*).

3. That on that date the respondent (*specify act, decision or omission to be reviewed*).

4. That the petitioner seeks (*state remedies sought*). The petitioner craves the court to pronounce such further orders (including an order for expenses) as may seem to the court to be just and reasonable in all the circumstances of the case.

5. That the petitioner challenges the decision [or act or omission] of the respondent on the following ground(s).

6. (*State briefly (in numbered paragraphs) facts in support of the ground(s) of challenge.*)

7. (*State briefly (in numbered paragraphs) the legal argument with reference to enactments or authority.*)

PERMISSION TO PROCEED

8. That the petitioner satisfies section 27B(2) (requirement for permission) of the Court of Session Act 1988. (*State*

[132] RCS r 58.3(4)(a).
[133] RCS r 58.3(4)(b).

briefly (in numbered paragraphs) how the petitioner can demonstrate a sufficient interest in the subject matter of the petition and why the petition has a real prospect of success.) [or

8. That the petitioner satisfies section 27B(3) (requirement for permission: second appeals test) of the Court of Session Act 1988. (*State briefly (in numbered paragraphs) how the petitioner can (a) demonstrate a sufficient interest in the subject matter of the petition, (b) why the petition has a real prospect of success and (c) either why the petition raises an important point of principle or practice or why there is some other compelling reason for allowing the petition to proceed.*)]

(*where an extensions to the time-limit under section 27A of the Acct of 1988 is sought*)

[8A. That the Court should allow this petition despite it being made after the period of 3 months beginning with the date set out in paragraph 2 because (*state why the Court should consider it equitable, having regard to all the circumstances, to allow this petition*).]

8B. That the following documents are necessary for the determination of permission [and extension to the time-limit]:

(*set out, in a numbered list, the documents required to be identified by rule 58.3(4)9d)*).

TRANSFERS TO THE UPPER TRIBUNAL[134]

9. That the petition is not subject to a mandatory or discretionary transfer to the Upper Tribunal. [*or*

9. That the petitioner is subject to a discretionary transfer to the Upper Tribunal under section 20(1)(b) of the Tribunals, Courts and Enforcement Act 2007] [*or*

9. That the petitioner is subject to a mandatory transfer to the Upper Tribunal under section 20(1)(a) of the Tribunals, Courts and Enforcement Act 2007.]

---

[134] For guidance on transfer to the Upper Tribunal, in particular the exercise of the discretion to so transfer, see *JR v Advocate General for Scotland* [2024] CSOH 64.

PLEAS-IN-LAW
(*Specify pleas-in-law relating to each ground of challenge and remedy sought.*)

According to Justice etc.
(*Signed by counsel or other person having a right of audience or, under 4.2(3)(ca), agent.*)

SCHEDULE FOR SERVICE
PART 1: RESPONDENTS
(*State the name and designation of the respondent(s) and whether service is sought in common form or by advertisement.*)

PART 2: INTERESTED PERSONS
(*State the name and designation of any interested person(s) and whether service is sought in common form or by advertisement.*)[135]

SCHEDULE OF DOCUMENTS
(*Specify any documents founded on under rule 58.3(4)(b).*)

A number of features about this are worth mentioning. First, there is no prayer or crave as such, nor do the remedies sought appear at the very beginning of the petition (as with a summons), nor at the end (as with any other form of petition). Instead, somewhat counterintuitively, they appear in statement 4. Second, the style specifically invites the court to grant such further orders as may seem just and reasonable; so, in granting a remedy, the court is not necessarily confined to the orders specified by the petitioner. Be wary however: if the application is made under section 45(b) of the Court of Session Act 1988 (seeking specific performance of a statutory duty), the precise terms of the order sought must be stated.[136] Third, the form not only invites but demands averments about legal argument with reference to authorities; anathema in traditional pleading. Fourth, there is a requirement for pleas-in-law (which at least, unlike the statement of remedies sought, appear in their traditional place, at the

---

[135] On service, remember to serve the petition on the Lord Advocate and the Advocate General for Scotland if a 'devolution issue' arises: Scotland Act 1998, Sch 6.

[136] *Carlton Hotel Co* v *Lord Advocate* 1921 SC 237.

end of the petition). Lastly and most importantly is the requirement for our old friend, brevity. This was emphasised by Lord Hope in *Somerville* v *Scottish Ministers*[137] where, after saying that the rules governing petitions for judicial review were intended to lay down a simple form of procedure capable of being operated with reasonable expedition, he went on to say this:

> As a result the degree of precision and detail in written pleadings that has traditionally been looked for in other forms of action in Scotland is not to be looked for in petitions for judicial review ... The core requirement is simply this. The factual history should be set out succinctly and the issues of law should be clearly identified. The aim is to focus the issues so that the court can reach a decision upon them, in the interests of sound administration and in the public interest, as soon as possible.

So (as with any pleadings): brief, succinct and focussing on the issues – good; verbose and woolly – bad.

Group proceedings

A detailed consideration of the procedure in group proceedings is beyond the scope of this book but we mention them here for the sake of completeness, since in many respects the procedure mirrors that in commercial actions in the Court of Session;[138] consequently the pleadings ought to be approached in the same way. Specifically, the summons must be in Form 13.2-AA.[139] It must have conclusions, specifying the orders sought;[140] identify the parties to the proceedings[141] (which in this case will include the 'representative party for the pursuers'

---

[137] 2007 UKHL 44, 2008 SC (HL) 45 at 69 per Lord Hope of Craighead.

[138] Group actions can be raised only in the Court of Session, by virtue of the Civil Litigation (Expenses and Group Proceedings) (Scotland) Act 2018 s 20(1); the procedure is regulated by RCS ch 26A.

[139] RCS r 26A.19(1).

[140] RCS r 26A.19(2)(a).

[141] RCS r 26A.19(2)(b).

rather than the 'pursuer' or 'pursuers'); specify any special capacity in which the representative party is bringing the proceedings or any special capacity in which the proceedings are brought against the defender;[142] summarise the circumstances out of which the proceedings arise;[143] and set out the ground on which the action proceeds.[144] The above advice about how to draft a commercial writ therefore applies equally to group actions.

Before a group action can proceed as such, permission must first be given for it to do so.[145] This requires an application for permission to be lodged with the court in Form 26A.9, along with 'the summons by which it is proposed to institute proceedings',[146] i.e. a draft summons. All we need say about the application for present purposes is that one of the grounds for refusing permission is that it has not been demonstrated that there is a *prima facie* case; so you will need to ensure that your averments do disclose such a case (and, for that matter, that the proposed proceedings have a real prospect of success).[147] While the court will not expect the finished article (as *Mackay*, referred to in the footnote, illustrates) there is a minimum threshold which your pleadings will need to meet if permission is to be granted.

Similarly, before a group action can be commenced, an advance application must also be made to the court, along with a copy of the proposed summons, for a person (the applicant) to be the representative party.[148] You will have to satisfy the Lord Ordinary that the applicant is a suitable person who can

---

[142] RCS r 26A.19(2)(c).

[143] RCS r 26A.19(2)(d).

[144] RCS r 26A.19(2)(e).

[145] 2018 Act, s 20(5).

[146] RCS r 26A.9(3)(a).

[147] RCS r 26A.9(3)(b) and (d). As to what these expressions mean in this context, see *Mackay v Nissan Motor Co Ltd and Others* [2024] CSOH 68 at paras 44 and 46 per Lord Sandison.

[148] RCS r 26A.5(1) and (7).

act in that capacity.[149] The matters to be taken into account include the special abilities and relevant expertise of the applicant; the applicant's own interest in the proceedings; whether there would be any potential benefit to the applicant, financial or otherwise, should the application be authorised; confirmation that the applicant is independent from the defender; demonstration that the applicant would act fairly and adequately in the interest of the group members as a whole, and that the applicant's own interests do not conflict with those of the group whom the applicant seeks to represent; and the demonstration of sufficient competence by the applicant to litigate the claims properly, including financial resources to meet any expense awards (although the details of funding arrangement do not require to be disclosed).[150] These matters do not have to be averred in the summons itself but you should be careful to take full instructions from your client so that you are in a position to satisfy the Lord Ordinary about them.

Summary applications

What is a summary application?

A summary application is a form of procedure competent only in the sheriff court. It is defined in the Sheriff Courts (Scotland) Act 1907:

> '*summary application*' means and includes all applications of a summary nature brought under the common law jurisdiction of the sheriff principal, and all applications, whether by appeal or otherwise, brought under any Act of Parliament which provides, or according to any practice in the sheriff court, which allows, that the same shall be disposed of in a summary manner, but which does not more particularly define in what form the same shall be heard, tried, and determined.[151]

---

[149] RCS r 26A.7(1).
[150] RCS r 26A.7(2).
[151] Sheriff Courts (Scotland) Act 1907, section 3(p).

The first step in knowing how to draft a summary application is understanding why your case falls to be dealt with by this particular form of procedure. Understanding the legal basis for your action being presented to the court in the form of a summary application is key to ensuring the application itself is in the correct format.

In general terms, summary applications arise in two situations:

(i)   Applications of a summary nature (i.e. requiring to be brought expeditiously without delay/unnecessary steps in procedure) under the common law jurisdiction of the sheriff court.

(ii) Applications brought/appeals made under a particular statutory provision.

Common law summary applications are rare. The most commonly encountered application (although still rare) is for authority to disinter and re-inter deceased bodies buried in cemeteries.[152] If you do have a common law application, it would be worth discussing the case with your local sheriff clerk depute and providing some advance notice of the impending application, and perhaps a cover letter on lodging the writ for warranting which sets out the basis for the application being raised as a summary application. Whilst it is your responsibility to ensure that your action is being raised in the correct format and never for the clerks of court to be advising you on form/procedure, given summary applications often require some degree of urgency in their disposal, providing as much information as you can at warranting stage will greatly assist the court and avoid unnecessary delay.

---

[152] However, see the Burial and Cremations (Scotland) Act 2016 and in particular, section 27 providing a new scheme (to be made by regulations not yet in force at the time of writing) for applications for public exhumation. For further discussion on examples of common law summary applications, see Macphail, *Sheriff Court Practice*, ch 26, paras 26.171 to 173; and G Jamieson, *Summary Applications and Suspensions* (2000) chapter 15.

It is much more likely that you will require to draft a summary application because your application/appeal is being made under a particular statute which either of itself, or by an Act of Sederunt, requires the matter to proceed as a summary application. As set out further below, the form of a summary application generally follows that of an initial writ.

Rules of procedure

Rules of procedure (including those relating to form) may be found in the principal statute under which your application proceeds.

Before putting pen to paper, you must scrutinise the particular legislation in terms of which your action arises to ascertain any particular procedure as to the form of the application, including checking the existence of relevant regulations or Act of Sederunt. You should of course already have consulted the legislation to ascertain the appropriate legal test and will therefore already have noted any particular form of procedure necessary.

Summary application rules

Helpfully, the majority of rules relating to summary/statutory applications of the kinds most commonly encountered are set out within the Act of Sederunt (Summary Applications, Statutory Applications and Appeals etc) Rules 1999. The various rules of procedure are beyond the scope of this text.[153]

As ever, you should pay particular attention to the time-limit for making your application. It may be subject to limitation provisions within the applicable legislation.[154] If your application is an appeal arising from a particular statutory provision, the time-limit for bringing your action may be contained within that statutory provision. If not, then your application must be

---

[153] See Macphail, *Sheriff Court Practice*, chs 26 and 27 for an excellent and detailed appraisal of same.

[154] See Macphail, *Sheriff Court Practice*, ch 26, para 26.37 for a helpful overview.

lodged within 21 days after the date on which the particular decision[155] appealed against was intimated to your client.[156] In addition, your application if concerned with rights or obligations may be subject to prescription.[157]

The pleadings
Initial writ
If you can draft an initial writ, you can draft a summary application. The majority of summary applications are made by initial writ.[158] The format looks the same, other than that above the words 'initial writ', the writ states that it is a 'summary application under' and then specifies the particular title and section of the statute or statutory instrument in terms of which the application is made. For example, 'SUMMARY APPLICATION IN APPEAL UNDER SECTION 28F(1) OF THE EDUCATION (SCOTLAND) ACT 1980'.

Instance
The parties should be designed in the instance in the same manner as an initial writ.[159] The person making the application is to be designed and referred to as 'the pursuer'. The person required to be called as a party to the application (the respondent) is designed and referred to as 'the defender'.[160]

---

[155] Or 'order, scheme determination, refusal or other act complained of' per 1999 Rules, r 2.6(2).

[156] 1999 Rules, r 2.6(2).

[157] Prescription and Limitation (Scotland) Act 1973, ss 6, 8 and Sch 1; see also Macphail, *Sheriff Court Practice*, ch 26, para 26.35; Jamieson, *Summary Applications and Suspensions*, paras 17-04 to 17-10.

[158] 1999 Rules, r 2.4, with initial writ in form 1. For examples of summary applications not initiated by initial writ, see Macphail, *Sheriff Court Practice*, chs 26 and 27, paras 26.47 and 27.25.

[159] No defender requires to be designed in an application under the Adults with Incapacity (Scotland) Act 2000; see 1999 Rules, r 3.16.7(1) and form 23; see also Macphail, *Sheriff Court Practice*, ch 26, para 26.50.

[160] 1999 Rules, r 2.1.

Craves and condescendence

Thereafter, the writ should contain craves setting out the orders sought from the court and a condescendence with numbered articles setting out the relevant facts on which the orders sought are craved. In terms of the rules, certain matters must be averred.

Where the pursuer has reason to believe that an agreement exists prorogating jurisdiction over the subject matter of the summary application to another court, the writ should contain details of the agreement.[161] Where the pursuer has reason to believe that proceedings are pending before another court involving the same cause of action and between the same parties as those named in the instance of the initial writ, the details of the proceedings should be set out in the writ.[162] In an action relating to a regulated agreement within the meaning of section 189(1) of the Consumer Credit Act 1974, there should be included in the writ an averment that such an agreement exists and details of the agreement.[163]

More generally, averments should include the ground of jurisdiction for the action and the facts on which that ground of jurisdiction is founded.[164] Like ordinary proceedings, where the residence of the defender is not known and cannot reasonably be ascertained, that should be averred in the writ, including the steps taken to ascertain the defender's whereabouts.[165] Similarly, if there are persons who appear to the pursuer to have an interest in the application, a warrant for intimation on such persons should be craved, and there must be included in the initial writ averments relating to such persons.[166]

Any particular averments required by the rules pertaining to the particular legislation in terms of which the application is made should also be specified.

---

[161] 1999 Rules, r 2.1(3).
[162] 1999 Rules, r 2.1(4).
[163] 1999 Rules, r 2.1(4A).
[164] 1999 Rules, r 2.1(5).
[165] 1999 Rules, r 2.1(6).
[166] 1999 Rules, r 2.1(8).

Pleas-in-law

Summary applications have pleas-in-law. It should be unnecessary for you to 'free style' here. The styles relating to the particular applications contain style relevant pleas-in-law. In any event, the general observations relating to the drafting of pleas-in-law should be observed.

Answers

Where the court orders answers, these follow the format in an ordinary action. The instance should follow that of the initial writ, for example 'ANSWERS FOR RESPONDENT IN APPEAL UNDER SECTION 28F(1) OF THE EDUCATION (SCOTLAND) ACT 1980'. Thereafter, they should contain all that defences in an ordinary action would contain. Adjustment, if permitted by the court, should be conducted as it would in an ordinary action.

Simple Procedure

As a trainee or newly qualified solicitor you are likely to work on at least one Simple Procedure action.[167] It may be passed to you under the (false) premise that, because this form of procedure contains the word 'simple' in its title and is designed to be utilised by those not qualified in the law, it will be uncomplicated. You may sense an expectation that you should just pick up the file, run with it quickly and ask as few questions of your supervisor as possible.

Two things about that. First, while Simple Procedure is designed to resolve low-value claims (claims under £5,000) as expeditiously and with the least expense to parties as is possible, you need to take care to comply with the rules of procedure (of which there are many) and to set out your client's position

---

[167] Simple Procedure was introduced by section 72 of the Courts Reform (Scotland) Act 2014 following the Report of the Scottish Civil Courts Review (2009); the rules of procedure are contained within the Act of Sederunt (Simple Procedure) 2016 (SSI 2016/200) ('Simple Procedure Rules').

in writing as clearly as possible. Secondly, despite being more 'user friendly' than other forms of court procedure, the underlying law applicable to the dispute is unchanged. The value of a claim does not affect the complexity of the law. Many complicated points of law can be found in low-value claims raised in the Simple Procedure court.

So, the same case analysis should be employed as in all other forms of procedure. What is your client hoping to achieve? What are the relevant legal principles? What are the facts relevant to prove your client's case in law/defend the action against them? Only when you have carried out that analysis should you start completing the Simple Procedure claim/ response forms.

Jurisdiction and procedure

The Simple Procedure rules govern, in general, claims in which the sum of money claimed is less than £5,000.[168] There are some exceptions to that general rule. For example, personal injury actions[169] and actions for the recovery of certain heritable property remain subject to the summary cause rules.[170] In addition, claims that ought to be raised in the tribunals system should be raised in that forum.[171]

---

[168] See Court Reform (Scotland) Act 2014, s 72(3); and for a full account of the proceedings subject to the Simple Procedure Rules, see Macphail, *Sheriff Court Practice*, ch 31.

[169] Summary Cause Rules, chapter 34; and see Macphail, *Sheriff Court Practice*, ch 24, paras 24.158 to 24.165.

[170] Housing (Scotland) Act 2001, ss 14 and 36; and Sheriff Courts (Scotland) Act 1971, s 35(1)(c) but with amendments pending per Courts Reform (Scotland) Act 2014, Sch 5, para 6, and in any event, restricted in scope by other statutory provisions depending on the nature of the property/removing. See Macphail, *Sheriff Court Practice*, ch 23, paras 23.05 to 23.67.

[171] For example, certain cases arising from private residential tenancies should be raised in the First-tier Tribunal (Housing and Property Chamber) per Housing (Scotland) Act 2014, s16, and Private Housing (Tenancies) (Scotland) Act 2016, s 71.

Although there is an upper limit of £5,000, there is no lower limit. Any claim under £5,000 is therefore competent. While very, very low-value claims for payment are rare, they should, pled correctly, result in the court being in a position to reach a swift resolution of the claim, possibly without a hearing. Some of the best and most memorable cases you will deal with in your career are likely to arise from the Simple Procedure forum. Dogs, cars, grass-cutting, defective second-hand toys, broken taps, a medium's unpaid fees... it is a fruitful source for a wide-variety of claims. While the subject matter may seem unimportant or trivial to you, it is likely a matter of great importance to the claimant/your client. The same care should be taken in the preparation of court documents in this procedure as in any other.

Before drafting your claim, you would be wise to consider the Simple Procedure Rules in full. In relation to how to draft a claim/response, particular attention should be paid to chapters 3 and 4 of same.

How hard can it be when it is supposed to be simple? A surprising number of claims (even those, maybe even particularly those, drafted by solicitors of many years' experience) fail to comply with the basic requirements of a claim and response form. There are many traps for unwary solicitors: adopting the same familiar form of pleading used in ordinary actions and ignoring what the procedure requires; or constraining your pleadings to the necessary forms, but at the same time failing to read the words telling you the information needed in a particular part of the form; or getting everything absolutely right ... apart from the designation of the respondent, thus producing a worthless, unenforceable order at the end of it all and having to start again. How then, can you avoid these pitfalls?

The same but different

In the Simple Procedure world, pursuers are referred to as 'claimants' and defenders are referred to as 'respondents'. The written notice of claim and defence (the pleadings!) are contained within forms prescribed by the rules. The claimant submits a claim form. The respondent submits a response form.

Initial writs and defences do not form part of this happy Simple Procedure planet. Everything is contained within the form.

The form, together with the rules and the guidance note, tells you exactly what you need to include in each section of the form. Despite that, a surprising number of cases fail to set out what is required.

First, and this cannot be stressed enough, *use the form.* The procedure is designed to be simple and straightforward. All of the information that you require to give to the court should be contained within the form. Very many litigants, particularly those represented by solicitors more familiar with the traditional form of pleading in the ordinary court, choose to pay little attention to the form, insert 'see paper apart' into every box and append to the form written pleadings in the style of an initial writ or defences. That practice should be avoided. Why? First, if your opponent is a lay person they may be confused and fail to understand the claim/response, thereby defeating the principles and purpose of Simple Procedure. Parties should be able to read the case against them in the form and style dictated by the rules. Alternatively, if your opponent is the respondent, they may take your lead – thinking that you, as a solicitor, must know best – and similarly append a paper apart to the form. That inevitably results in a very lengthy and unfocussed defence, causing unnecessary extra work for you and your client. Secondly, you should be mindful of the person ultimately adjudicating upon your case: the sheriff! Simple Procedure produces a high volume of cases for the sheriff court. Every case requires to be reviewed by a sheriff when a response form is lodged in order to manage the case and issue the written orders required. Opening a claim/response form to see every part answered with 'see paper apart' requires the decision-maker to locate and open on a case management system a further separate document. It is unnecessarily time-consuming. A paper apart should only be utilised when you have genuinely run out of space on the form. In forms completed electronically, that situation should arise infrequently, particularly given the brevity implied by the procedure.

The claim form

The claimant is obliged per the rules to set out certain matters in the claim form, namely the identity and address of the parties, the essential factual background to the dispute, what the claimant wants from the respondent if the claim is successful, why the claim should be successful and what steps have been taken to resolve the dispute with the respondent.[172] Helpfully, the claim form, divided into sections A to F, is organised in a format directed to these matters.

The orders

After preliminary boxes for completion with the name of the particular sheriff court, the name of the claimant and name of the respondent, Part A requires you to state what orders you want the court to make if you are successful (the craves in traditional pleadings). As with any form of pleading, to complete this section you must have a clear idea about the orders competent in law that the court can make if you are successful.

The full particulars of the parties

Parts B and D require you to design the parties. Simple Procedure requires the same precision when designing the parties as any form of action. Any order granted in your client's favour will be issued against the respondent as designed by you in Part D of the claim form. If you have designed the respondent incorrectly, the order granted in your client's favour will not be capable of being enforced. Taking care at the outset will avoid the embarrassment of having to confess to your client that even 'simple' procedure has eluded you.

What's it all about?

Part E is the background to the claim. Think 'E' for 'essential' rather than 'everything'. In this section, the claimant is asked to 'briefly describe' the 'essential facts' behind the claim and why the claim should be successful. As with articles of condescendence in an initial writ, only the facts necessary to prove

---

[172] Simple Procedure Rules r 3.3.

the claim/justify the granting of the orders sought should be included. The kitchen sink approach should be avoided. But remember you need to provide enough information to support the claim. Simple Procedure is sometimes misunderstood as a process permitting 'scant pleadings'. For example, if you are founding on breach of contract as the basis for your claim, you will need to set out that the parties entered into a contract, refer to the relevant contract terms (and possibly incorporate the contract), describe the way in which that contract has been breached and specify the loss has been caused by the breach. Insufficient information runs the risk of the court dismissing the action at the outset, or an 'unless order' requiring you to correct your mistakes which failing the court will dismiss the action.

In Part E2 you are indicating (by tick box) why the court has jurisdiction to decide the claim. Any basis of jurisdiction not founded in the first three options (events taking place in the court's district; respondent residing in the court's district; agreement as to jurisdiction) needs to be stated under 'other'.

A separate part of the form is dedicated to consumer credit agreement claims. The form tells you the information to include in the background information (section E4).

Steps to settle the claim

Part E5 contains an important section, and one that will be carefully scrutinised by the sheriff. What steps have you taken, if any, to try to settle the dispute with the respondent? The words 'if any' are a little misleading. If you simply answer this section to state that no steps have been taken, the court will want to know why. There may be a good reason as to why no steps have been taken to settle the dispute. However, such situations will be rare. The rules encourage early settlement of disputes (including settlement before raising a court action).[173] If you haven't tried, the court is likely to direct you to discuss the case in order to attempt to settle it or at least narrow the

---

[173] Simple Procedure Rules rr 1.2(4) and (5), 1.4(3) and (4), 1.5(5) and (6), 1.8(2).

issues genuinely in dispute. Alternatively, you may be ordered to proceed to mediation.

The response

The general principles set out above apply equally to the response form. Certain matters must be included in the response form and again, the form is directed to your including those matters.[174] The substantive parts of the response form are as follows.

Part C directs the respondent to state whether they wish to admit the claim or dispute the claim. C1 should only ticked in the event that the respondent accepts the claim against them and wishes to resolve/settle the claim before the last date for a response per the timetable issued along with the claim. If the claim is admitted, there is no need to complete Part D. The claim ought to be settled by the respondent, and thereafter the action is disposed of either on the claimant's application or by the court.[175] If the claim is not settled by the last date of the response, it is open to the claimant to submit an Application for a Decision within the timescale prescribed by the rules asking the court to grant what the claimant has asked for in the claim form (i.e. to grant decree).[176]

If the claim is admitted but the respondent wants time to pay in terms of either the Debtors (Scotland) Act 1987 or the Consumer Credit Act 1974, box C3 is ticked, and at the same time a Time to Pay application in form 5A is sent to the court.

If any part of the claim is disputed, box C2 is ticked and Part D1 completed. Part D1 is the section in which the substantive defence should be outlined. Like the claim form, sufficient detail should be included to set out what is admitted, what is denied and any further essential facts required to prove a relevant defence in law. Simple Procedure does not allow a respondent to 'reserve their position' although many response forms seek to do just that. Nor does it permit a response as

---

[174] Simple Procedure Rules r 4.4.
[175] Simple Procedure Rules r 7.2.
[176] Ibid.

follows: 'The claim is denied. The sum sued for is excessive'. In terms of rule 4.4, the respondent must set out in the response form which facts (if any) are agreed with; which facts, if any, the respondent disagrees with and why; and why the respondent thinks that the claimant should not get what was asked for/ only some of what was asked for in the claim form. You must comply with that requirement; otherwise, you run the risk that decree will be granted at written orders stage, or otherwise an 'unless order' requiring further specification, which failing a grant of decree.

The response form also allows the respondent an opportunity to set out the steps taken to resolve the claim. If none have been taken, the court may order parties to discuss matters or send the case to mediation. If you/your client has taken no steps to resolve the claim, as well as setting that out at Part D2, you may wish to include you/your client's willingness to enter into such discussions.

Counterclaims

Unlike in ordinary cause procedure, the Simple Procedure rules do not allow a counterclaim to be made by the respondent. It is open to a respondent to raise a separate action against the claimant in respect of any sums due to the respondent. The absence of a counterclaim mechanism is something to bear in mind at the point in time you are discussing/negotiating a settlement with the other side. It is another reason to seek to resolve the action before court proceedings if necessary.

Other aspects of drafting in Simple Procedure

There are no 'motions' or 'minutes' in Simple Procedure. If you need the court to make an order in your client's favour you should use the appropriate forms to do so. Some aspects of procedure have their own dedicated form, for example in the event of the respondent failing to lodge a response form timeously, an Application for a Decision (form 7A) should be completed and lodged (rather than a Minute for Decree).[177] An

---

[177] Simple Procedure Rules r 7.4.

Additional Orders Application is the way in which you ask the court to grant any order not already catered for by a specific form.[178] For example, if you want to pause the action for settlement or fix a particular hearing, or change the timetable in some way, you would use this form.

It is competent for a claimant to ask the court in a Simple Procedure case to grant an order before a final decision is made in the case in order to protect their position; in other words, an application for interim diligence.[179] Again, the form directs you as to the information required in respect of each type of order sought, including the important *why* the court should be making the order sought.

Whatever order you are seeking, completion of the relevant application form is a form of pleading. It gives notice to the court and your opponent as to the application you want the court to grant and why. Importantly, it contains the points to which your submissions will be anchored during any hearing. Focussing your mind as to the relevant legal principles in support of your application on the eve of a hearing is too late. When drafting any application, stand back and ask yourself if you could explain to the court now, based on the completed form, why it should grant the order. If the form doesn't contain information relevant to do that, more work is needed.

    … Simples!

---

[178] See Part 9 of the Simple Procedure Rules.

[179] Arrestment on the dependence under section 15A (1) of the Debtors (Scotland) Act 1987; an inhibition on the dependence under section 15A (1) of the Debtors (Scotland) Act 1987; interim attachment under section 9A (1) of the Debt Arrangement and Attachment (Scotland) Act 2002.

CHAPTER SIX

Ethical Pleading

Duty of candour

It has been said that,

> Our whole system of pleading and disposal of cases upon
> preliminary pleas must depend upon each party stating with
> candour what are the material facts upon which he relied and
> admitting the facts stated by his opponent which he knows to
> be true.[1]

Given everything we have said in the preceding chapters, we
would hope that that does not come as a surprise. For the lawyer, candour is everything. Candour with the court. Candour
with your opponent. Candour with your client. You have
already been told that you must have an evidential basis for
your averments. You should also already know that you must
have a basis for denying the other side's averments. But it is
worth re-emphasising this point.

Your client may wish to scream into the void and attempt
to resist the inevitable. Your client may even ask you to 'just
say it didn't happen'. But if you know that the position you
have been asked to plead is not true, then you must not plead
it. That is the case whether you are pursuer or defender. That
does not normally mean that the defender requires to volunteer

---

[1] *Ellon Castle Estates Co Ltd v Macdonald* 1975 SLT (News) 66 at 66 per
Lord Stewart.

to the pursuer that which she does not know or to point out additional evidence which may assist the pursuer's cause. Of course it doesn't mean that. But what it does mean is that if a particular statement of fact is pled by the pursuer, then it is the defender's duty to admit, not know and not admit or deny that fact – and to do so truthfully. While there may be certain situations in which it is acceptable, on ECHR grounds apart from anything else, to do no more than to 'test' the other side's case (e.g. if you are acting for the parent responding to a local authority's application for a permanence order to be granted in respect of their children), in the vast majority of civil cases the defender is not entitled simply to deny the pursuer's averments and to put the pursuer to proof. To do so would amount to an abuse of process, in breach of the duty of candour, and will likely see the defences dismissed as irrelevant. As Lord Justice Clerk Gill put it:

> We do not accept that, by pleading a bare denial, the appellant is entitled to an enquiry in which the respondents are put to the proof of their averments. The court has repeatedly deplored that sort of approach.[2]

So remember, if you are to act in your client's best interests, you must get them to engage with the process, which includes being candid. If you are to act in observance of your duties to the court, you must never plead something you know to be untrue or which is not and which will not ever be vouched by evidence. And if you are to act in your own self-interest, you will remember that the court and the other members of your profession have long memories, and that sharp practice will never see you right in the long term. If a case, or a defence, is unstateable, you must never proceed with it.

---

[2] *Urquhart v Sweeney*, 2006 SC 591, at para 42 per the Lord Justice Clerk (Gill).

Evidential basis for averments

It should go without saying, but we will say it anyway, that you must never aver a fact for which you have no evidence. As Lord Justice Clerk Moncrieff said in *Boustead v Gardner*,[3] with massive understatement:

> It is a fraud in itself to make statements which are made in the hope that something may turn up in the course of the case to justify them; when this statement was put on record, the party who did so did it on chance. I do not think that is a style of pleading which should be encouraged.

Not only should such pleading not be encouraged, it is liable, pretty swiftly, to your losing the trust of the court forever, or being struck off, or both; rightly so in each case. So, never do it. Provided that your client has not told you that he is lying, it is not necessary that you personally should believe the version of the facts that you are averring. But there must *be* evidence which entitles you to make every averment in your conde-scendence, whether that is to be found in a precognition, witness statement or document. Do not let your enthusiasm and your quite natural belief in the justice of your client's case run away with you. Even if there is some evidence vaguely support-ing an averment, on a practical level you do not want to plead your case too high: if the evidence at the proof does not come wholly up to some of the averments on record, that may make the judge suspicious of the rest of your case.

If you have no evidence for an averment, and it is not cru-cial to your case, then there is no harm in not making it. If the averment is crucial, then you must carry out, or instruct, further investigations to establish whether evidence can be found in support of it, before the averment could be pled. If that evidence cannot be found then the case was doomed to fail anyway.

[3] (1879) 7 R 139 at 145.

Sometimes, one finds that parties try to get round this rule in a variety of different ways, none of them to be recommended. Suppose that a pursuer's case rests on proving that a bribe was paid by the defender's employee, X, to the pursuer's employee, Y. Unless there is evidence that a bribe was paid, for example, a statement by Y that a bribe was paid, or CCTV footage showing a brown envelope clearly labelled 'bribe' being handed over by X to Y, you could not aver that it was. That would not be cured by an averment of the sort one sometimes sees: 'the pursuer believes that X paid a bribe'. The pursuer's belief is irrelevant and if you did make such an averment it would not, or certainly should not, be admitted to probation following a debate (or would otherwise attract unfavourable judicial comment at a case-management hearing). Nor, without more, would a bald averment 'believed and averred that a bribe was paid' solve the problem of lack of evidence.

However, the requirement for evidence does not mean that there must be *direct* evidence. If there are facts, of which you do have evidence, from which an inference could fairly be drawn that a bribe was paid, then after averring those facts, you could legitimately plead either that a bribe was paid, or at the very least, make a 'believed and averred' averment to that effect. For example, if one witness spoke to a brown envelope being handed over, and another to an email passing between X and Y speaking of 'sweeties' being paid, and there was evidence of Y doing work on X's house at a reduced price,[4] you would be entitled to aver those facts, followed by an averment that a bribe was paid, because that fact is capable of being inferred from the facts of which there is direct evidence.

In a passage which might fairly be described as Delphic, Lord President Carloway has attempted to explain when a straightforward averment could be made, and when it must be preceded by 'believed and averred':

---

[4] This example is drawn from *Oil States Industries (UK) Ltd v "S" Ltd* [2022] CSOH 52, 2023 SC 209 where, on not wholly dissimilar facts, the court did infer that a bribe had been paid.

The pleader may have confused the circumstances in which the formula 'believed and averred' can, and in rare cases ought to, be used. There is a significant difference between a situation in which a party can only prove certain facts, but an inference can be drawn from those facts (where the formula may be used) and one where the party has circumstantial evidence from which fraud is, by inference, proved. In the latter, a straightforward averment is appropriate.[5]

What that appears to be saying is that an averment of a particular fact may be made if that fact can be inferred from circumstantial evidence; but that if the fact can be inferred from other facts, you must aver those other facts, in which event the formula 'believed and averred' may be used. On one level it is possible to see what is meant. If, in a damages action, you require to prove that the defender's car was being driven at excessive speed, and there is evidence that it left the road on a bend, you could legitimately aver that the car was being driven at excessive speed, without preceding it by 'believed and averred', although you would also be well advised to aver that the car left the road. On the other hand, it is difficult to see that there is any real difference of substance between being able to prove certain facts, from which an inference may be drawn, and circumstantial evidence (presumably, proving certain facts) from which an inference may also be drawn. If nothing else, fair notice would appear to require that averments be made of the facts from which it is said that an inference can be drawn

In considering all of this, and deciding whether an inference can be drawn from primary facts or not, you will (as so often, when drafting pleadings) require to exercise your professional judgment. We can do no better than adopt and adapt the advice routinely given to juries in criminal trials: any inference that your pleadings invite the court to draw must be reasonable and based on facts for which there is evidence; what you must

[5] *Marine & Offshore (Scotland) Ltd v Hill* [2018] CSIH 9, 2018 SLT 239, at para 17 per the Lord President (Carloway).

not do is speculate or guess about matters on which there is no evidence.

The lesson to take from all of this is that there must be an evidential basis for every averment that you make, even if the evidence is indirect, from which an inference may fairly and properly be drawn. Standing Lord Carloway's observations, provided you are satisfied that an inference may be drawn, you need not use 'believed and averred'.

When an expert report is required

You do not necessarily require to have all your evidence in place before raising an action or even before making averments, if there is other evidence to support the averments made. For example, in a damages action arising out of a road traffic accident, you would be entitled to aver that the defender was driving at excessive speed for the road conditions, if you had eye witness evidence to that effect, without having in your possession a report from a collision investigator, even if you might choose to instruct such a report before the proof. However, it follows from the requirement that you must always have some evidence to support every averment you make, that there are some situations where you must have an expert report before making averments, and one of those is where professional negligence is alleged. Averments of professional negligence must have a proper foundation. It is not enough for your client to say, or for you to aver, that his previous solicitor failed to implement his instructions. The issue for the court will be whether the course taken was one that no solicitor exercising ordinary skill and care would have taken, and for that to be averred, you ought to have a report from a suitably qualified expert which supports the making of such an averment.[6] (There might be some limited situations where you might justifiably make averments of professional negligence, and indeed proceed to proof, without having an expert report

---

[6] *Tods Murray WS* v *Arakin Ltd* 2011 SCLR 37.

– see the opinion of Lord Sandison in *Cockburn* v *Hope*,[7] where he expressed the view that there may be circumstances where the court is able to determine a question of professional negligence without an expert report – but in general, you would be well advised to get an expert report before making averments of professional negligence.)

In clinical negligence cases, you are likely to need not only a liability report for each medical professional being blamed, but also an expert report dealing with causation. Remember that in the clinical negligence context it has been described as a professional duty not to advance pleadings without proper investigation and support from an appropriate expert or experts who have carried out an expert assessment.[8] In general, if you wish to aver any fact which you will be able to prove only by leading opinion evidence on a matter which is not within the everyday knowledge of a lay person (or the judge) then an expert report is likely to be required before you can properly make the averment.

Pleading fraud

To paraphrase Mr Punch on the subject of matrimony, advice to pleaders thinking of pleading fraud: don't. Or, at least, think very carefully before you do. You would be well advised to read the cautionary words of Lord Hodge in *Grant Estates Ltd* v *Royal Bank of Scotland plc*,[9] referring to various well-known authorities[10] on the need for clear and specific averments of fraud. In particular, clear and specific averments are needed on three matters, namely (a) the act or representation founded upon, (b) the occasion on which the act was committed or

---

[7] [2024] CSOH 69.

[8] *JD v Lothian Health Board*, [2017] CSIH 27, 2018 SCLR 1 at para 54 per Lady Clark of Calton.

[9] [2012] CSOH 133 at para 87.

[10] *Shedden v Partick* (1852) 14D 721, *Kaur v Singh* 1998 SC 233, *The Royal Bank of Scotland plc v Holmes* 1999 SLT 563 and *Wright v Cotias Investments Inc* 2001 SLT 353.

the representation made and (c) the circumstances relied on as yielding the inference that that act or representation was fraudulent. Lord Hodge went on to quote Lord Brodie in *Zurich CSG Ltd* v *Gray & Kellas* that 'fraud is not something to be lightly inferred. Nor should it be lightly averred',[11] going on to comment that allegations of fraud can have very serious consequences for people, particularly those engaged in regulated professions, and can blight careers, at least temporarily, even if they are eventually not substantiated. Lord Hodge invited counsel to bear in mind these considerations, and so too should you.

That all said, you may also wish to look at what Lord Carloway said in the *Marine & Offshore* case,[12] where the Inner House did accept, allowing a reclaiming motion (appeal) from the commercial judge, that averments from which fraud could be inferred (although, presumably, not lightly inferred) would suffice. This is something of a minefield. On the one hand, voluminous averments are not needed simply because fraud is being averred. On the other hand, you still do need to give fair notice of precisely what the case based on fraud is, and there may be a fine line between circumstances where an inference of fraud may, and may not, properly be drawn. The best advice we can give is that your averments make clear precisely what acts and/or representations are being founded on and when they occurred, and are set out with sufficient precision, detail and clarity to justify an inference that fraud did indeed occur, as well as giving fair notice to the other side of what facts you are going to attempt to prove.

'Beating' a time-bar

In Chapter 2, we provided some tips on how to analyse your case. As part of that process, we recommended that you learn by rote the prescription or limitation periods that apply to the

[11] [2007] CSOH 91, 2007 SLT 917 at 923.
[12] *Marine & Offshore (Scotland) Ltd v Hill* (n 5).

most common types of claim. The purpose of that is so that you can identify, at the outset, the date by which the action must be raised in order to beat the statutory time-limit. Hopefully, that time-limit will not expire for at least a few months, and preferably longer, during which time you will be able to conduct all necessary investigations, take precognitions from all relevant witnesses, remind yourself of the law in the particular area and correspond with the would-be defender's agents – all before you start the process of drafting a relevant and sufficiently specific writ.

But what if your client first consults you on a Monday and it is clear that his claim will time-bar on Tuesday? In that case, you must forget about the niceties. The writ that you draft may not be a masterpiece of the pleader's art. Indeed, it may contravene most of the accepted canons of draftsmanship. But in such an earth-shattering emergency, it is always better to get *something* into court in order to beat a time-bar.

A few points to bear in mind if find yourself in that suboptimal situation:

1. If there is more than one potential defender and you simply can't work out which one is the right one, sue them all and let the wrong ones out later (but quickly).
2. While defenders may have the luxury of lodging skeleton defences, a pursuer cannot really lodge a skeleton writ. Even in the few hours that you have, aver enough so that the defender at least knows who the pursuer is, what event in the dim and distant past has prompted him to raise proceedings and what it is that the defender is said to have done wrong.
3. At the very least, try to get clear in your mind the basis of the action so that no attempts are made, however much in vain they may ultimately turn out to be, to argue that you only defeated the time-limit as against one ground of action (e.g. contract) but not another (e.g. delict).[13]

---

[13] See *Sellars v IMI Yorkshire Imperial Ltd* 1985 SC 235 and the cases discussed therein.

4. If the action time-barring imminently is a professional negligence action, you will have no chance of obtaining a supportive expert report. If you don't even have time to pick up the phone to an expert and to get their provisional assessment based on a succinct summary of the facts – or if the case is just too complicated for that – you will simply have to break with protocol and aver that the solicitor/architect/doctor has been professionally negligent and obtain a report, hopefully supportive, (immediately) thereafter.

5. Remember that at this stage, all you are trying to do is to beat the time-bar. Remind yourself of the overarching function of the writ: to give fair notice to the defender of the pursuer's case. So long as you keep this in mind, and keep a cool head, you should be able to bash something out[14] to preserve your client's position.

If you find yourself in this far from ideal professional situation, you should make it clear in correspondence with the defender that you are raising the action in order to defeat a limitation or prescriptive period and that you intend to have the action sisted to allow both parties time to investigate. That is particularly important in cases of professional negligence; in that event, you should be up-front with the defender's agents and inform them that you are without a report currently but that you will be instructing one immediately. So long as you stick to averring what you can and are candid with the defender about the position you are in, you should not find yourself in professional difficulties. You will be acting responsibly by getting a time-barring action into court in order to preserve your client's position.

Acting for public authorities

Those who act for public authorities, in particular those acting for branches of government, have heightened duties incumbent

[14] This is the only occasion in which bashing is acceptable.

upon them. Whether you prefer to analyse this heightened duty by reference to the 'duty of candour' or the 'rule of law' or, in appropriate cases, through the prism of the Human Rights Act 1998 matters not. The point to attest is a short one.

Public authorities do not have the privilege of acting like a private individual. While the individual is entitled to take every single point available to them (i.e. every stateable argument), the courts will have less time for public authorities adopting a similar tack. Public authorities ought, in general, to act as the model litigant. That means a number of things. It means taking a sensible and pragmatic approach to technical errors in the other side's pleadings, e.g. not taking a pleadings point that the defender has not been designed properly. It might mean taking a more helpful approach to informal requests for information in the course of a litigation, being proactive in the disclosure of documents (even those which may harm the authority's case) and providing 'willing and candid cooperation'.[15] And it might see the public authority giving far more assistance to a party litigant opponent than would be expected, for example, of an insurer.

If you are instructed by a public authority, do not simply presume that your client will want you to adopt the 'bulldog' approach that has got you your stellar reputation. That might, in fact, be the last thing that your client wants. If in doubt, take instructions, and if tempted to take what might be seen as a 'clever point', take instructions again.

If asked why you are so doing, you need point your client – who should know better – no further than this *obiter dictum* of Lord Drummond Young:

> I should observe that it has become commonplace for public bodies, whether the Scottish Government or local authorities, to raise preliminary objections at an early stage to appeals to the Court of Session by private individuals on the basis of standing or other factors. I do not doubt that in some cases

---

[15] *MacFayden v Scottish Ministers* [2024] CSOH 82, 2024 SLT 962 at para 22 per Lord Sandison.

such a course is entirely justified. Nevertheless, it is important that excessive use of preliminary objections should not be used to prevent the court from hearing substantive argument in cases that may have an important bearing on questions of public law, questions relating both to what the law is and to how it should be applied in a particular case. I would reiterate the renewed emphasis on the importance of the rule of law in public law decisions, and the fundamental principle that all forms of government, by any public body, must be conducted in accordance with the law. For that reason I would caution against the excessive use of preliminary objections to cut down appellate litigation.[16]

---

[16] *Taylor v Scottish Ministers* [2019] CSIH 2, 2019 SLT 288 at para 18 per Lord Drummond Young.

CHAPTER SEVEN

Beyond the Pleadings

All of the principles in the preceding chapters relate to the process of drafting written pleadings in the traditional sense. However, there are many forms of writing that form part of the advocacy in any court process. Any writing that finds itself before the court should be drafted according to the general principles in the preceding chapters. The following sets out some of the common forms of writing lodged with the court and guidance for same.

Emails – beware

The COVID-19 pandemic changed forever the way in which writs/documents are lodged with the court. Physical 'court runs' (attending at the sheriff clerk's office/General Department) are now largely a thing of the past. Lodging by email is now commonplace. While that may be a positive development for busy court practitioners and general convenience, be aware that your cover email may also find its way into the court process, and therefore before the sheriff/judge considering your case. Avoid simply attaching the document you wish to lodge in process to a long email chain exchange with the clerks. Keep it simple and keep it clean! If you wouldn't want the decision-maker or any other party to see what is in your email, don't send it.

The same goes for any communication with the court in which you are enquiring about a particular position, or commonly, asking for assistance from the clerks in relation to a point of court procedure. These emails may be forwarded to the sheriff/judge. Do you really need to ask the clerks the question? Or could you just look up the rules yourself and work it out? Remember, while clerks are very experienced sources of information on court rules and procedure, it is not their job to tell you how to do your job. Inevitably, they may simply forward your enquiry on to the decision-maker to ask them how to respond. Do you really want that to happen? And if you do need to ask the question, would you be happy if the sheriff/judge/other party to the action saw the email? These communications may find their way into the court process. If you do need to email the court, do not assume that the email will be responded to and deleted. Keep any communication with the court professional and concise and only include what is relevant.

Motions

In both Court of Session and sheriff court actions, certain applications require to be made by written 'motion' (i.e. applications in accordance with chapter 15 of the Ordinary Cause Rules and chapter 23 of the Rules of the Court of Session). They give notice to the other side and to the court of the application you are making. If the motion is opposed and a hearing fixed, it will be the focus of the hearing, and all submissions confined to what is intimated in the motion. So, it is important that it properly sets out, with precision, what it is that your client is applying for and why.

It is unnecessary to set out in this text the many and varied forms of motion that you may require to make to the court in this text. *Green's Litigation Styles* contains a useful bank of the most commonly encountered motions.[1] Do look at these styles before putting pen to paper. If you find yourself drafting a motion not covered by any of these styles, perhaps think again and consult a colleague as to the competency of what you are asking the court to do. While it is possible that you might

---

[1] *Green's Litigation Styles*, chapter E05.

properly be making the first motion of its kind in Scotland, it's also possible (more likely probable, particularly in the early days of your career) that you might be doing something completely incompetent. Best to check.

In general terms, a motion is in the form set out by the court rules.[2] After the instance, and the date, the body of the motion is structured as follows:

(i)   Your surname
(ii) Who you are acting for
(iii) What you are asking the court to do
(iv) Why you are asking the court to do that

So, for example: 'Johnston for the Pursuer, moves the court to discharge the diet of debate fixed for 1 January 2025 and thereafter to sist the cause for settlement to be implemented'.

Minutes

Many applications are required by the rules to be made by Minute. Substantive pleadings are found in any applications requiring to be made by way of Minute and Answer (see the general comments in the context of family actions). For the drafting of Minutes of Amendment see Chapter 4 above. However, many applications made take the form of a Minute. It is impossible to cover them all. Again, *Green's Litigation Styles* contains nearly form of Minute you may require to make.[3] Generally, the document, after the designation of the particular court, is headed up 'Minute of/for' followed by a description of the Minute you are making. For example a Minute of Sist, Minute of Abandonment, Minute of Tender, etc. It is followed by the instance and thereafter (although it varies depending on the nature of the application) the name of the solicitor/counsel

---

[2] In the sheriff court, form G6 per OCR r 15.1(b), and in the Court of Session, forms 23.2 and form 23.1C depending on whether the motion is enrolled by email or not: see RCS r 23.1C and 23.2.

[3] *Green's Litigation Styles*, chapter E03.

for the pursuer/defender followed by what is being stated to the court/applied for.

Written submissions

In any debate, at the conclusion of evidence at a proof/proof before answer or in respect of a complicated/lengthy opposed motion hearing, you may be ordered to lodge or you may volunteer to lodge and rely on written submissions. In other words, a written outline of your arguments in support of your client's position. The scope of this book is pleadings, not advocacy, but once again, it would be helpful to follow the general principles applied to the pleadings. Written submissions should be clear and only as long as is necessary. They should be clearly structured and well set out – paginated, paragraph numbers, at least line spacing 1.5 and font size 12… and if you really want some brownie points, give 'Palatino Linotype' a whirl.[4]

You are seeking to persuade the court to find in your client's favour. In order to make your arguments as attractive as possible to the reader, like any good story, your submission should have a beginning, a middle and an end. In general, an introduction; your motion/what orders you invite the court to make; the relevant legal principles to be applied by the court; the way in which those legal principles apply to the facts of the case and why those legal principles mean your client should be successful.

Lengthy written submissions referring to every known reported case on the particular circumstances should be avoided. Cite only the cases that are necessary. It may be very interesting that a particular principle has been applied by many courts far and wide, but do all those cases help your argument? Or can you simple rely upon the 'foundation case' in which the principle was established? The court is unlikely

---

[4] The prescribed judicial font.

to entertain a very lengthy list of authorities. Indeed, rules of court may restrict the number of authorities.[5]

Above all, remember:

> You are there to help the judge, not kill him through mental anguish occasioned by reading the unreadable and irrelevant.[6]

---

[5] For example, Sheriff Appeal Court Rules r 7.10.
[6] I Morley, *The Devil's Advocate*, 3rd edn (2015) p 158.

Index

EU representative:
Easy Access System Europe
Mustamäe tee 50, 10621 Tallinn, Estonia
Gpsr.requests@easproject.com

www.ingramcontent.com/pod-product-compliance
Lightning Source LLC
Chambersburg PA
CBHW061250220326
41599CB00028B/5602